RAVE REVIEWS FOR A TEEN-AGE AUTHOR

"Freckle-faced Cynthia was certainly no stereotype of the American girl that films and press had led her Indian school-mates to believe. Peace in the world doesn't seem so far off when one shares her discovery of how alike the young of all nations are."
—New York Herald Tribune

"Vivid, intelligent and provocative."
—New Yorker Magazine

"She writes like Mrs. Roosevelt and has the same heart. She is a happier representative of Western youth today than, shall we say, Francoise Sagan."
—Saturday Review

"Fine reading for young adults."
—Virginia Kirkus

"A book which is utterly charming."
—Christian Science Monitor

D0937473

WILLOW BOOKS

Leisure-time reading
Leisure-time pleasure!

Other WILLOW BOOKS you'll enjoy

AT HOME IN
INDIA

●

CYNTHIA BOWLES

▲ PYRAMID BOOKS ● NEW YORK

Written in the hope that the children of the world may one day grow up with a desire to understand the people now unknown to them, that they may one day grow up without losing the natural trust in their hearts.

AT HOME IN INDIA

A PYRAMID BOOK

Published by arrangement with Harcourt, Brace and Company, Inc.

PRINTING HISTORY
Pyramid Book edition published November 1959
Willow Book edition published April 1965
Second printing, September 1965

WILLOW BOOKS are published by Pyramid Publications, Inc.
444 Madison Avenue, New York, N. Y. 10022, U.S.A.

Contents

Preface

IN OCTOBER of 1951 my mother and father, younger brother and sister, and I left our home in Connecticut for India. I was fifteen.

I did not go as a student of India. I did not go to learn of its religions, its customs or its economic development. Nor did I go to India to compare it with America or to judge it in any way.

I went to India as a young, teen-age girl anxious not so much for knowledge as for the happiness and security which I was reluctantly leaving behind me in Connecticut.

Consequently this is not a book of facts and figures about India. Nor does it present generalizations and prophecies. It is a story of what I did in India, of the places I visited, and of the people I came to know.

I lived in India for almost two years. Much of this book was written during that time. In letters and a diary I recorded my impressions for my friends in America. Here, edited, I present them to you.

The purpose of this book is twofold. First, I write because I wish to share, as best I can, my experiences in India with you. I hope I will be able to show you a picture of India as I saw it. I hope you will be able to feel that my friends are your friends.

Second, I write in the hope that you will conclude, as I do, that my Indian friends are much like boys and girls in America and indeed all over the world. I believe that an awareness of the great similarities between us and all people, rather than of the superficial differences, is one of our greatest hopes for peace in the distrustful world of today.

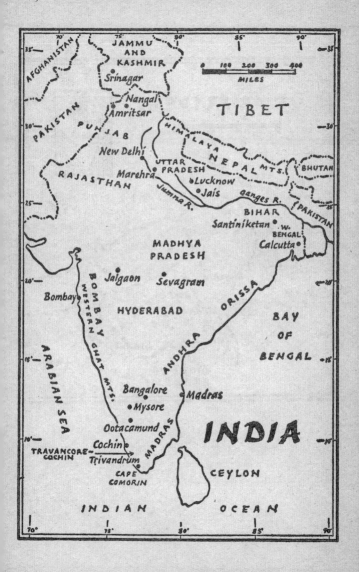

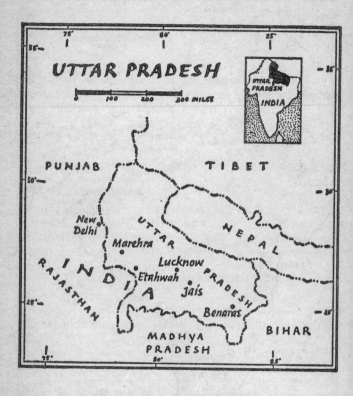

ONE

Whispers of India

I$_T$ WAS in July of 1951, when I was fifteen, that I first realized I might go to India. Stretched out in a hammock on the porch of the home in New Hampshire where I was babysitting for the summer, I noticed in the newspaper I was reading:

"BOWLES MAY BE SLATED FOR INDIA POST"

I was taken aback. It is true that the possibility of my father being appointed to a job in the foreign service was not new. During the spring he had been offered the ambassadorship to another country, and some time before our school vacation began and I left for New Hampshire, the question of the ambassadorship to India had come up. However, thinking the possibility a mere rumor, I had never taken seriously our family discussion on the subject. The announcement in the newspaper was clearly more than a rumor and I suddenly realized that my father's appointment was very probable.

At once several thoughts ran through my head. If my father were going to India would my brothers and sisters and I go with him? What would a home in India be like? Would we go to school there? These questions remained unanswered until I returned to my home in the small town of Essex, in Connecticut, at the end of the summer.

My father, whom almost everyone calls Chet, was fairly certain that his appointment was settled. He had always had a deep interest in Asia and firmly believed that it would be in India and the countries of Southeast Asia that the history of the coming generations would be made.

In September Chet's appointment by President Tru-

11

man was formally announced. My mother, my brothers and sisters and I each reacted quite differently to the idea of leaving Connecticut for India. Some years ago, after her graduation from college, my mother had spent several weeks in India and she was anxious to go back. But we had moved often in the last few years and she was sorry that we would have to move again so soon, without giving my younger brother and sister and me a chance to settle down.

My older brother and sister, both of whom are married, found it impossible to leave their jobs and families, but were both very envious of our opportunity. Sally, my younger sister, who was then thirteen, was eager to go and as impatient to leave as my father. Sam, my younger brother, then twelve, was happy in school here but was excited about going to a new country, especially one where he could learn new sports.

I, more than anyone in the family, was unenthusiastic. In fact, I did not want to go. It was not that I did not want to see India. I simply did not want to leave my home town, my school and my friends. The previous year we had come back from Hartford, Connecticut, where we lived for a year and a half while my father was governor. In September I had begun my sophomore year in high school and had just really settled down. I had good friends and I thought that if I went away again I might lose those friendships which I valued so much.

At the same time I knew that such an opportunity would probably never come again and I feared that I would later regret it if I decided not to go. Moreover, I had the guilty feeling that I ought to be enthusiastic about being so very, very lucky as to have the opportunity.

Fortunately, the decision was not given to me to make. My parents, sensing my indecision, decided for me, and although I was later grateful to them, at the time I was disappointed. My Essex friends told me afterwards that when I learned I was going away I came into school, silent, with my arms folded, a complete picture of gloom. So I started off to India on the wrong foot.

My father's appointment needed approval by a majority of the Senate. Until the vote was taken, on October 9th, our home was in a complete state of confusion and uncertainty. There were innumerable things to be packed— our clothing, our books, small furniture, chinaware, bicycles and musical instruments. Some of these were to be sent by ship, others by air freight, and a few things which we would be needing on our trip we kept aside to be packed in small suitcases. The house was littered with trunks and suitcases and duffle bags, and often with relatives and friends helping my mother pack.

Our packing was interrupted by frequent trips to the doctor's office for physical examinations and countless immunization shots against typhoid, typhus, tetanus, cholera, and yellow fever.

On the evening of October 9th we heard that the senators had finally approved my father's appointment and at last the trunks and suitcases could stay packed, goodbyes could really be said, and the plane reservations for October 13th could be confirmed.

Once our going was certain and the general confusion had let up a bit, I often found my mother, whom the Bowles family and almost everyone else call Steb, engrossed in some book about India or Asia. Her recollections of her visit in 1927 were vague and the books she read—Nehru's autobiography, John Muehl's *Interview with India*, Louis Fisher's *Life of Gandhi*, and others— helped refresh her memory and gave her an introduction to modern India.

We all tried to read and learn as much as we could about India in the short time that remained before we would arrive there. Sam and Sally and I knew very little. Of course we had heard of Gandhi when he died in 1948 and of Nehru when he took Gandhi's place as the leader of India. We knew little or nothing, however, of India under the colonial domination of the British. We knew little of the independence movement and we were only vaguely aware of the extraordinary strides that had been made since India had become a self-governing state in 1947.

We had heard of the big cities of Bombay and Calcutta but we had no knowledge of the villages, which we later learned are the real heart of India.

We had heard of the poverty, of the teeming, hungry millions, but we had heard almost nothing of India's new leaders who are so determined to erase the poverty. Nor had we any idea of the great number of village workers who have real hope for a better life for the Indian population.

We had heard about India's snakes and snake charmers, her holy men and maharajas, whose importance people, we found later, very much exaggerated.

We had heard of India's heat and grime but somehow missed hearing about the months of spring-like, sunny and cloudless weather. People had understated the beauty of her gorgeous flowers and birds, her peaceful villages and, above all, of her graceful people.

Sally, Sam and I had the good fortune to be able to go to India and to prove to ourselves how incomplete our ideas on India and Asia were. I feel that there must be some way—perhaps increased study of the countries of Asia in American schools, perhaps the setting up of Indian information service offices and libraries in more American cities—to erase the misconceptions of the millions of Americans who are not likely to have the wonderful opportunities we had. For these are the small misconceptions which, added together, so often prevent real mutual understanding, and consequently promote distrust and hate between the peoples of the world.

A document called the Post Report which we received from the State Department about a week before we left America did not add to our understanding of India. This was a report made up by people in the American Embassy in India, which was sent to all diplomatic personnel before their arrival in India. It contributed, probably more than anything else, to India's reputation in narrow, European-oriented diplomatic circles as an "uncomfortable place to get stuck in." It described India's climate, food, diseases, social customs and diplomatic protocol in what we discovered to be greatly exaggerated terms, and advised those going to India what to bring in the way of clothing, food and medicine. Even my father began to feel grim about taking Sally, Sam and me there. We were later ashamed of our uncertainties.

Along with the Post Report we received a few photographs of the "bungalow" in which we were going to be living in New Delhi. We could tell little from the pictures except that it was a one-story house, decorated and furnished much like any American home. There was a living room, dining room, kitchen, library-office and three bedrooms.

So, knowing little of India except what the Post Report told us, and wanting very much not to leave home, I went to school daily, silent and resentful, grimly saw my friends, came home and dutifully packed, until October 13th when we left.

The morning of October 13th dawned bright and beautiful. Small white clouds floated lazily in the otherwise clear blue sky and the sun was warm and comforting. It shone brightly on the woods around our home and on the trees on the banks of the river, accentuating the red, yellow and orange in their leaves. Gulls flew low over the water crying mournful songs, and a convention of southbound grackles, who were taking rest in the field outside my window, chuckled amiably.

This is what I saw and heard when I woke that morning. I looked across the cove to the sun-brightened town and wished very much that I were not leaving it and the beauty around me.

By 9:00 a.m. our house was filled with last-minute well-wishers. We all tried to pretend that this day was like any other. Yet inside we know that it was very, very different and it was difficult to restrain our feelings, of excitement and, in my case, unhappiness, at going so far away.

At 11:00, after final goodbyes to our friends and to our numerous dogs and cats, we left our home—the house on the bank of the river—and Essex, our town, and, after two hours on the road, we left Connecticut, our state.

I can remember little of what was said or done between the time we arrived at the airport and when we left on the non-stop Paris plane at 4:00. I remember only that we checked the baggage and verified our passports and had a final visit with our remaining family and friends who had come to New York with us. Then it was time to go and we went up the boarding steps and onto the plane.

Soon after, the plane took off with a great roar and we went higher and higher and farther and farther away from our friends and home.

At midnight a few days later, after quick stops at Paris, Geneva, Rome, Cairo, Basra, Iraq and Dhahran, Saudi Arabia, the stewardess announced that we were coming into Bombay.

TWO

Hello to India

We STEPPED wearily down off the plane and into the hot Bombay night. The smiles with which we greeted the kind people who had waited until the early hours of the morning to meet the plane were, I am afraid, somewhat uncertain, and Sally's, Sam's and mine faded completely as soon as we found the dark privacy of the back seat of the car which would take us into the city to a hotel. We were to have a few hours sleep there before the Embassy plane left for Delhi after breakfast.

The ride from the airport into the city and on to the fantastically big and elaborate Taj Mahal Hotel on the Bombay harbor took about thirty minutes. For hours I had been worrying about this first view of India. Just what would India be like? I knew so very little about her.

I had heard repeatedly, however, of her miserable poverty. To me extreme poverty was something abstract, unreal in a way because, although I had seen it, I had never come close to it. The thought that it was people who bore its terrible burden and children who shared it with them was somewhat frightening.

Finally, while on the plane I had thought, "Why don't you stop thinking about what India may be like and wait until you get there? Expect anything and you will not be shocked or frightened."

So I was not entirely surprised when, on each side of the road, we passed hundreds of men, women and children sleeping on string-bottomed cots, rug-like mats and the cement of the sidewalks.

It was very hot that night and I concluded that it must be cooler to sleep outside than within the stuffy walls of a house. But there were few substantial houses in sight, far too few for the hundreds of people whom we saw sleeping. Even the roughly constructed shacks that lined parts of the road could never have housed them all. I realized that many had no home except the road, no bed other than the sidewalk and no other roof than the sky.

But I was tired, and did not worry long that night about the poverty we had seen and how it could exist side by side with the luxurious hotel to which we were going.

The Taj Mahal Hotel is a massive, Victorian-looking building on Bombay harbor. Barefoot servants showed us down the wide marble corridors to our huge, high-ceilinged rooms. After a quick look at the moonlit harbor outside the window we were soon all asleep.

Four hours' sleep refreshed us remarkably. The day was fresher too. The rays of the bright hot sun sparkled on the little waves in the harbor and brought out the colors in the flowers in the garden beneath our window. The street was alive and awake, already bustling with early morning activity.

After breakfast we went back to the airport along the same road we had travelled not many hours before. The poverty remained. But the drabness, the dreariness, the deathly stillness of the night was gone and an aliveness, a freshness, and a bustle of human activity had taken its place. Laughter, talk and shouting had taken the place of the silence of the night. And color, the bright, gay hues of saries which the women wore so gracefully, had taken the place of the drab greyness we had seen so recently.

On the sidewalk, which we had last seen covered with

immobile forms, mothers were busy preparing the morning meal, men were getting ready to go to work or were already at work, young girls helped their mothers and tended their small brothers and sisters, and children laughed and played. Farther out of the city we saw boys and young men, aided by small mongrel dogs, bringing herds of cattle, sheep and goats into the city to market.

I realized more completely then that the word poverty is not an abstract term. The very essence of poverty is people—real people, eating, walking, talking people—human beings who live and suffer and have emotions of love, of happiness and of sadness, human beings little different from those I had always known.

Soon we were seeing the city from the air and then we headed northeast for New Delhi. Most of the way between the two cities we passed over clusters of small houses, the villages of India. Surrounding each village lay brownish green fields. Occasionally we could see a river, winding its way across the land.

A few hours later we landed at the Delhi airport. But long since our lack of sleep had caught up with us, and we were drowsy and hot and, after our Bombay initiation, terribly uncertain what our new home would be like. More than anything else we all wanted a cool shower, a little sleep and a feeling of being settled.

Waiting to greet us when we stepped off the plane was a crowd of photographers and reporters and a long reception line of people from the American Embassy, an overwhelming and unexpected welcome.

One of the friendliest faces that emerged for Sally, Sam and me from the new unfamiliar, uncertain world into which we had all stepped was that of my father's driver, a big, kind, good-natured man. His name was Jewan Singh and he drove us the six miles that day from the airport into the city to our new home at 17 Ratendon Road.

As it was the middle of the day, and very hot, there were not many people along the road into the city. We passed a couple, walking with huge bundles balanced on their heads, and a man cycling with another man sitting side saddle on the rear fender. We easily overtook a big cart pulled by two slow-moving, hump-backed cattle which Jewan said were called bullocks. But most of the people whom we passed were resting at the side of the road in the shade.

There were few villages along the way. Most of the land was dry and rocky, dotted with numerous bushes and occasional trees.

As our home-to-be was located on the nearest edge of New Delhi, we saw little of the city that day. But what we saw was modern and clean, like parts of Washington, D.C., we thought. My father told us that New Delhi had been built up as the capital of the country within the last twenty years.

I was glad for my "expect-anything" attitude once more as we turned into the small driveway of 17 Ratendon Road. I noticed at once that the house was unpretentious and home-like, for which I was very glad. But stiffly lined up on the front steps were eleven men, dressed in white uniforms with elaborate red, white and blue decorated turbans and wide red, white and blue belts. They were introduced to us as our servants.

One of the men, whom we gathered was a head butler, and who was called Shakur, stepped forward, greeted us warmly and took us into the house. It was wonderfully cool inside, as the house was air-conditioned. We liked our new home even though it seemed much too tidy and unlived in. We met the rest of the servants, most of whom spoke English, had our lunch, strictly American style, and began to unpack.

In the days that followed we settled into our new surroundings. But for weeks my brother and sister and I were not happy in these surroundings. We felt uncomfortable and strange. Outside the house I felt that I was in a world which, although friendly, seemed somehow remote from reality.

When we moved to Hartford I had felt much the same. All I was sure of was myself, my family and my home. Everything else was uncertain and almost unreal.

The Americans whom we met during those first few

weeks in Delhi seemed as strange to me as the Indians. Both groups seemed so different from people we had known at home. I soon found that a great shell was growing up around me, out of which I knew I must crawl if I were to be happy.

As the days passed, the weather gradually became cooler and the evenings were lovely. We often took walks around the neighborhood and in the beautiful park in back of our home. Ratendon Road was a quiet, shady, little-travelled street. An occasional car or truck, creaking bullock cart or cheerfully jingling two-wheeled, horse-pulled tonga cart broke the quietness at intervals. Men passed on their bicycles, hurriedly or slowly, depending upon their temperament and destination. Sometimes I could hear the happy chatter of small children in a language I did not understand.

Our neighbors on one side were members of the Chinese Embassy. On the other side lived an Indian family whose children soon became good friends of Sally, Sam and myself. Across the street lived the family of an American who worked at the United States Information Service. An Indian doctor and his family also lived opposite us. His son and Sam became inseparable.

In time I grew to love Ratendon Road. I came to associate it with sounds and sights that I shall never forget. But for those first few weeks, although Sally, Sam and I learned to accept our new surroundings and our new life as we had accepted environments we had gone into as strangers before, we did not understand them. Without understanding we could never be happy. We had a lot to learn.

One thing we learned to understand but could not easily accept was the presence of so many servants. We were a small family and the house was not big. We were used to doing things for ourselves. Consequently we did not enjoy having, and felt it was unnecessary to have, someone to drive for us, someone to shop for us, someone to cook for us, someone to serve us at the table, someone to tidy up for us and someone to water the garden for us. We soon realized that our American beliefs in informality and equality were stronger than we had ever imagined. We felt uncomfortable having the servants doing all our work and accepting us as their superiors.

But we soon learned that most Indians believe that they are born into a particular occupational group, social class or position, and they are generally unwilling to do the work of one of a lower status. We learned also that this belief, and with it the whole caste system in India, is rapidly becoming more flexible. Indeed, the entire caste system has been legally abolished.

However, in the case of the servants, each would do only his special kind of work. Thus, the washerman would not cook the food, the cook would not wash the clothes, the butler would not work in the garden, the gardener would not wait on the table, and so on. And if we, who were respected and regarded as having a superior status, interferred and did some of the work ourselves, the servants would resent it, feeling either that we were criticizing the way in which they had done the work, or that we were degrading ourselves.

When we got to know the individual servants better, we explained to them how we lived in America, how Americans do much or all of their own housework and how they have invented gadgets and machines to make their housework easier. After that they better understood and less resented our insistence on doing so much of our own work. Later we found equally good jobs for some of them in other homes.

This understanding on their part came slowly, and certain of the servants only grew accustomed to us without ever really understanding our American ways. Once I was playing with some of the servants' children in the little courtyard of the compound in back of our house where they lived with their parents. The ball we were playing with fell into the drain that led to a ditch outside in the back alley. Lila, one of the younger children, ran over with me to get it, and I noticed, as I had many times before, how dirty and slimy the drain had become.

"Wouldn't it be fun if we could make this nice and clean?" I suggested to Lila.

"Oh, no, Bahenji,"* she said. "You mustn't do that kind of work."

"It would be fun, not work," I said. She said "Accha," which means okay, and we started in scrubbing.

All went well until the wife of Jewan, the driver, came along. She was horrified to see us hard at work, hands muddy and faces dirty. Other grownups came running, scolded us soundly and told me to stop immediately and get clean.

"That is not your work," they told me. "It is Madan's." (Madan was the sweeper, the person of low caste who did all the dirty work.)

But the head butler, Shakur, came into the compound just then and explained: "In Bahenji's country people don't mind getting their hands dirty." And then he went on to tell them what he had come to understand about American ways.

Shakur, Jewan and the other servants were a great help in urging me out of my shell. In time they became some of my very best friends.

THREE

Back to School

SOON AFTER we arrived in New Delhi, the question of school came up. Sally, Sam and I felt very much like fish

* In Hindustani, the language of the majority of North Indians, *Bahenji* means respected sister. *Bahen* means sister and *-ji* is a suffix denoting mixed respect and affection which can be tacked on any proper name or title. Thus Gandhiji, Punditji (Prime Minister Nehru is usually referred to in this way), and Mataji or Pitaji (meaning mother and father, used as terms of respect for elderly people). I referred to women whose names I didn't know or whom I knew and because of their age or position I was meant to respect as Bahenji. Most of the persons whom I later worked with called me Bahenji.

out of water and homesick in our new surroundings. We thought that school and its new friendships might bring us that understanding which would make us feel happier and less out of place.

We felt that for the next year or so our formal education was relatively unimportant. We could learn geometry and Latin anywhere but learning about India was an experience which could come only through such a rare opportunity as we had, and we wanted to make the best of our good fortune.

With this thought in mind we began to inquire about the schools in and near Delhi. Most of the Americans whom we asked suggested Woodstock School, an excellent boarding school located in the beautiful foothills of the Himalayan mountains, about three hundred miles north of Delhi. This was the school to which almost all of the Americans living in northern India sent their children of junior and senior high school age. It was run principally for Americans and the courses offered were similar to college preparatory courses in an American high school.

But we learned that not more than a quarter of the students there were Indians, and that the teachers and staff were predominantly American. At Woodstock we would be able to continue our formal high school education and thereby have no difficulty in entering a college in America when the time came. But we would be learning little of India and as far as conventional education was concerned could just as profitably have stayed at home in Connecticut.

An Indian woman whom Steb met at the Embassy suggested one of the Indian convent schools in New Delhi or Delhi. There were two of these schools, both run by Catholic missionaries. Although they were good schools they were terribly overcrowded, and the secretary was not encouraging when Steb asked if we could be admitted.

As we were limited to schools which taught in English, there were just three more which we could consider. The Lady Irwin Secondary School for Girls was good and specialized in teaching home economics which Sally and I thought would be interesting. But because all three of us wanted to go together we decided on a co-educational school.

The Modern School, also in New Delhi, was progressive, not patterned after the conventional English school. Its curriculum included subjects which, unlike the strictly college preparatory subjects which most of the other schools offered, appeared to me more fitting for a generation whose job it is to build a free and poverty-less India. Unfortunately we were incorrectly informed that the Modern School taught only in Hindi, the principal language of northern India, and we felt that this eliminated us, at least for the several months that it would take to learn the language.

The school which we finally selected was called the Delhi Public School. It was really not a public school in the American sense, since there was a charge of twenty-five rupees (about five dollars) a month. It was co-educational and conveniently located, about two miles away from our home. It also was overcrowded. However, the classes were conducted in tents which would be put up and taken down as the enrollment of the students fluctuated.

At the time we entered Delhi Public, the teachers and all the thirteen hundred students were Indians, with the exception of a wonderful family of Indonesian children who later became our close friends. These were students of many religions: Hindus, Moslems, Sikhs, Buddhists, and Christians. The principal was an Englishman who was alternately pleasant and impressively stern. He ran the school as he might have run a private school in Great Britain.

I remember clearly the first day that we went to school. Two boys who lived next door and who went to Delhi Public School were already good friends of my brother Sam, and the three were off on their bicycles by 8:30. School began at 9:00, so Sally and I started out soon after.

As our bicycles from home had not yet arrived, we had rented some from a bicycle dealer in Connaught Place, New Delhi's very much westernized market place. The bikes were rather old and we had not gone far when

Sally's chain came loose. Not being experienced in fixing bicycles, and, moreover, being somewhat frightened in our venture out into a world with which we were still very unfamiliar, we became quite alarmed.

Should we walk the bikes home and get Shakur to help us fix them (in which case we would be late for school on our very first day), or should we walk them the rest of the way to school? In this state of uncertainty, another of Sam's new-found friends, on his way to school also, recognized us, and asked if we were having any trouble. We showed him the chain and were terribly embarrassed when he fixed it in a flash. Thanking him, we continued on our way, reaching school just in time. We parked our bicycles with the hundreds of others and went to our respective class tents.

Apparently the word had already gone around that three Americans were joining the school. I had been admitted to the senior-most class which was equivalent to the sophomore or junior class of an American high school. There were about fourteen boys and six girls in the class and the girls were already there when I arrived. We had a minute before the teacher came in which we said shy hellos and introduced ourselves briefly.

When the girls saw our class teacher, a stern-looking, oldish woman, coming, they told me to go quickly to my seat. I stood with the rest of the class as the teacher came into the tent, arranged her papers and sat down, but could manage only a completely surprised look when the boys and girls chorused, "Good morning, ma'am."

The excessive formality with which the students at Delhi Public School treated the teachers was completely new to me, and I am afraid that I never really became accustomed to it. It always irked me that we, in typically childish fashion, pretended such great respect for the teacher while she was present but did what we pleased behind her back or when she was absent from the tent.

After the attendance had been taken we formed into a line like ten-year-olds and walked to an open space behind one of the tents where the whole school was gathering in a semi-circle for prayers. When we were all quiet, our English principal said a prayer and then led the school in saying two more, one of which was the Lord's Prayer. But we were young and the prayers had not originated with us. Like parrots we repeated the words without thinking and behind "ma'am's" stern back we winked at each other and braided each other's hair, though not on that first day, of course.

After prayers, my first class was a games class in which we played a game very much like basketball. This was followed by geography, then Indian history, and finally English grammar. All of these subjects were compulsory.

A little before 12:00 we had a three-quarters of an hour break for lunch. The girls had all brought, or had their family servants bring, a box lunch, Indian style. Shakur had packed a few sandwiches and some apples for my brother and sister and myself. I ate my share of them while my new classmates ate curry and dhal and chappatie, a kind of unleavened bread.

The girls were anxious to hear about America. The first question they asked me was whether I had ever seen a movie star. (I had. Jane Russell was on the same plane we had been on from New York to Paris.) Similar questions followed and I answered them as best I could, although I soon realized that they knew more of Hollywood than I did.

I found it hard to make myself understood. The English of most of the girls was perfect. But mine was anything but perfect and was well punctuated with the incomprehensible American slang. To all appearances we were talking two very different dialects. However, within a month or so I had learned to speak Indian English and my friends had become more accustomed to my American English.

After lunch we had four more classes. The first was a course called Scripture in which the Bible was analyzed. This was an optional subject and most of the students took chemistry and physics at this time. Chemistry and physics were taught together as the last year of a two-year course, so I, not having had either before, took Scripture instead.

After Scripture we had mathematics which was also too advanced for me. I later received special help in geometry during this period. Math was optional too and some of the girls took homemaking and hygiene instead. During the next to the last period we had art and lastly, Hindi.

Then our classes were finished for the day and the girls took me on a tour of the school grounds. All the school activities, except the small clinic, were conducted in tents. The tents in which classes were held were big enough to seat thirty comfortably. They were without lighting, fans or windows but were completely open on one side.

The principal and vice-principal's tent was smaller and well equipped with electric lighting and a fan, as was the administrative office. In another small tent was a store where books, paper, pencils, pens, etc., could be bought. Next to this was the tent in which the sports equipment was kept. Another tent was the library and another a store where you could buy candy, fruit and ice cream and delicious fried food.

The clinic was a small, dome-shaped stone building, wonderfully cool, built by the Moslems in the fifteenth century, probably as a tomb.

Perhaps it is hard to imagine a school in tents. I came to like it very much. Although we were often too hot in summer and too cold in winter we always had fresh air and I liked the closeness to nature.

All sorts of wildlife visited us. Little chipmunk-like squirrels loved to scamper up the tent ropes and patter across the roof of the tent. Birds of all kinds were constantly flitting in and out, and big black and white hawks circled above the school, casting huge shadows on the ground. One day I saw a mongoose, a weasle-like snake-killer, peer around the corner of the tent and then slink quickly away.

On the edge of the school grounds there were two big fields, one for soccer, hockey and cricket and the other for netball, a game like basketball. Nearby were two smaller fields for volleyball and badminton. Two of the younger classes were playing hockey when we went by.

The school was on the very edge of the city, and that first day when we climbed a small hill to get to the clinic, the surrounding countryside was almost deserted. It was mostly flat but dotted here and there with rocky hillocks, a few stunted trees, and many small green bushes. Before I left India new houses and apartment buildings had been built up all around the school.

It was almost 4:00 before my new friends walked me over to the bicycle park (they went home by school bus) and I said a still shy but much happier goodbye. When we reached home, Sally, Sam, and I agreed that life in India was really not so grim after all. Although we had dreaded venturing out into our new surroundings and meeting people our own age, we were glad that we had. We were sure that studying at Delhi Public School would be a happy experience for us.

In the months that followed I found that I was constantly comparing Delhi Public School to the high school that I had gone to at home. I have already mentioned the formality and strictness of the Delhi school. In their method of teaching the two schools were also very different.

In our Indian history class at Delhi Public School, for instance, we were expected to learn by following, in our own books, the passages that the teacher was reading out of her history book. There was no discussion, no questions. The teacher added little to what was written in the book. It was a drill, not a lesson.

In most of our other classes we were taught in the same way. Our art work consisted of copying, in color, the drawing the teacher had made on the blackboard.

This kind of unoriginal teaching was hard to get accustomed to. I found the classes boring and uninspiring. But I am sure that had I been intent on really learning and getting high marks, I could have learned as much as I would have had I been at home.

Another great difference between the schools at home and Delhi Public was the method of examining. In Essex we had occasional tests throughout the year, but had no final exam. We were marked on the basis of the tests and on the class work and homework we had done. At Delhi Public School we had frequent, usually weekly, tests and a final exam made up by Cambridge University in England. Many of the students failed and had to repeat the exam the following year.

Delhi Public School was not a typical Indian high school. The fact that it was co-educational set it apart from the great majority of high schools in India. It is not customary for girls and boys of high school age to study together.

Yet except for its co-education, Delhi Public School could probably be called typical of a certain group of Indian high schools. Most of these schools were established during the British rule, usually by British schoolmasters and are similar to high schools in Great Britain thirty years ago.

They are supported and run by private individuals or groups, charge a tuition of from three to ten dollars monthly, teach in English, and prepare the students for the Senior Cambridge or a similar examination. Their curriculum is similar to a college preparatory curriculum in the United States. Of the greatly insufficient number of high schools in India, most are still of the kind I have just described.

In India at present, public education is by no means as developed as in America. However, most state and local governments have helped to build elementary schools and a growing number of secondary schools in their areas. These differ from the Delhi Public School type of school in that they were founded after independence, are government supported, charge little or, more usually, no tuition and generally have a lower standard of English or teach in Hindi or the regional language. They prepare the students for an examination made up by state or local examiners. The curriculum of these schools is sometimes college preparatory but more often includes such courses as homemaking, agriculture, and crafts.

The Central Government realizes the inadequacy of the old educational system. Although more than half of the younger children even in the villages now go to school, there are schooling facilities for only ten per cent of the children between the ages of eleven and seventeen.

The directive of the Indian Constitution is that free and compulsory education shall be provided for all children up to the age of fourteen. To meet this demand and the demand of the children themselves, schools are rapidly being built in villages, towns and cities throughout India. The predominantly village population of India is fast growing literate. There will, I hope, always be villages in India but the new country is showing in this great effort that there need not always be illiteracy, that illiteracy and the people of the villages need not always be synonymous.

FOUR

A New Friendship

SAM, SALLY and I each felt differently about Delhi Public School. But we agree now that the friendships that we made there were the happiest and most valuable part of our experience in the school.

Although she was unlike me in every way, I came to know and like the best a pretty, outgoing girl named Suman. I remember that the first day I went to school she was the most outspoken and curious of all my classmates.

Just as I had formed a stereotype of Indian girls before I came to India, she had apparently formed a stereotype of American girls, largely from the numerous Hollywood movies she had seen. Therefore, she was a little disappointed that I, the first American her age she had ever really known, didn't act, talk and look as she had expected American girls to. But she was anxious to be friends and often, in the first few weeks of school, went out of her way to do things with me.

About a month after I started school, Suman introduced me to the movies in New Delhi. The Rivoli Theater is very near Connaught Circle, the wealthier class's main shopping center, and we went there from school on the school bus. The theater was already crowded mostly with what Suman identified for me as college students and young, yet to be employed, graduates. There were few girls and I felt conspicious and self-conscious in my American clothes and wished that I were wearing Suman's loose-fitting salvar and cumeez.

The salvar is an ankle length pantaloon affair, with a draw string at the waist that gathers in the two yards of material. It is usually made of white cotton material although sometimes of the same material, color and print as the cumeez.

Cumeez means shirt in Hindustani. The cumeez is very much like a man's shirt in that it is loose-fitting around the waist, but it is designed more like a dress and is worn over the salvar. Like the American girl's dress, the length, color, material and style differ with each person.

Suman usually wore a bright-colored, big print cotton cumeez which reached to her knees. Long cumeez were the fashion at that time and most of the school and college girls wore them down to, or a little below, their knees.

In addition to the salvar and cumeez, the Delhi girl wears a kind of shawl, called a chunni or dapatta, of light-weight material, about six feet long and two feet wide, which drapes around her shoulders and down her back or over her head as she likes.

The salvar and cumeez is the dress typical of the Punjab, a province just north of Delhi. But recently it has been adopted by many girls throughout India to take the place, in sports or work, of the more cumbersome sari.

That day at the movies, Suman, who I think would look beautiful no matter what she wore, was looking particularly lovely in a light and dark green cotton print cumeez with white cotton salvar and chunni. She was wearing lipstick, which just a few, more westernized, older girls have begun to wear, and had braided her jet black hair into two long braids. She had several jingling glass bracelets on each wrist and I felt quite conspicuously inferior to her as we went into the theater and up to the ticket window.

The theater was much the same as any movie theater in America although, I must say, more plush than any I had seen near our home in Connecticut. There were three groups of seats, each having a different priced ticket. If you bought a cheap ticket for one rupee, four annas (about 25 cents), you would sit right in front of the screen. Even this cheapest ticket is out of the reach of most Indians. The most expensive ticket was 3/12 (about 75 cents), and the ticket which we and most people bought cost 2/8 (about 50 cents).

We bought some coke and potato chips and went into the theater to listen to the music, both Indian and popular American, and wait for the show to begin.

There were three short newsreels, one that centered on Indian news, one on world news, and another that featured news in the United States. Next there were various advertisements and a cartoon, and then Hollywood's *Francis Goes to the Races.*

Many Hollywood movies are shown in New Delhi and the other big Indian cities. I seldom went but when I did it was usually with Suman who, like many upper-income Indian girls, went almost weekly. At one time or another I saw *Come Back Little Sheba, Gas Light,* with Ingrid Bergman, *Scaramouche* and a Bob Hope picture.

It is primarily on films such as these that most Indian movie-goers base their ideas and opinions of America. I remember being horribly embarrassed by certain scenes in *Come Back Little Sheba,* in which a high school boy acted aggressively toward his girl friend and was not very firmly repulsed.

In America I would have enjoyed the movie. I would not have given any thought to those particular scenes. But sitting in the New Delhi theater, I realized that I, unlike the other movie-goers, understood the attitudes that it portrayed. Without this understanding the Indian movie-goer could only attribute to Americans a great lack of modesty and morality.

However, *Come Back Little Sheba* was by no means the worst of the films Hollywood regularly sends to Delhi and other Indian and Asian cities. For example, some of our westerns, which often show a rough and arrogant attitude toward American Indians, while bad enough in the United States, looked much worse in New Delhi. Not only do these films give Indians false ideas about what American life is like; many of them present a picture of wealth and luxury so far out of the average Indian movie-goer's experience that he concludes, as one of my pen-friends did, that America is a "paradise on earth." The Hollywood movie serves as a kind of escape from the less attractive realities of his own environment.

There is yet another and perhaps more constructive reaction that these movies produce. Indian teen-age and college-age boys and girls see American young people enjoying a close and natural companionship, going to school, church, parties and dances together. This causes them to think about and to become discontented with the restrictions which the caste system, the joint family and the general high moral standards of their society place upon them.

Italian movies too are popular in India, and just as misleading. Suman and I saw *Bitter Rice* and *Bicycle Thief*. In February of 1952 the International Film Festival was held in Delhi and we saw Japanese and Russian films.

The Indian movie industry itself is the largest in the world outside that of U.S.A. With Suman and other of my friends I saw quite a few Indian films. Most of these, in their length, and variety and number of calamities—birth, death, marriage, illness and accident following one upon another—resembled Hollywood's *Gone with the Wind*. Many were a rather unsuccessful combination of comedy and tragedy. They exaggerated Indian life just as the Hollywood pictures do the life of America, and often they dwelt at great length on India's proud past.

I had long hoped to see an Indian wedding, so I was happy when one day toward the end of January Suman asked me if I would like to go to a wedding of a friend of hers. The wedding was to be the following night and Suman told me that she would pick me up early in the evening.

I was ready at 5:00 when she drove up. Suman was wearing a sari and looked wonderfully grown-up. The sari was silk, light pink, and had hundreds of tiny silver sequins sewed to the end that fell from the shoulder. She wore large sparkling earrings and a lovely plain gold bracelet.

In America such elaborate jewelry would suggest great wealth. But Suman's family was not particularly wealthy. Jewelry, even gold and silver, is relatively inexpensive in Delhi and it is customary for girls, even of families of modest incomes, to own expensive-looking pieces.

We drove through the crowded Delhi streets, past the parks filled with families and groups of young students, taking their rest from work and study as they do throughout the world, and across the city to the bride's house. Since the house was deep in the heart of Old Delhi, on a dirty, very narrow, crowded street, I was surprised to find the home large and comfortable and the people inside it English-speaking. When we arrived the house was already crowded with friends and relatives of the bride. We were taken into a room where some of the women and girls were sitting and talking.

Among them was the bride-to-be, dressed in her beautiful red bridal sari and not yet acting shy. As soon as the groom and his friends arrived she would have to assume an expression of shyness and modesty. Her closest relatives sat near her, continually fussing over her, fixing her sari or the brilliant flowers in her hair.

I thought of the newly-wed bride I had seen at a wedding reception Suman and I had gone to just a few weeks before. She had acted very shy, keeping her head bowed and her eyes lowered. I later learned that this shyness may have been genuine. But genuine or not, it was what was expected of her. She was married and had just entered a new household. She could no longer act as a young girl but must act as a modest, dutiful young wife should.

Women guests had come up to her one at a time, with a small gift or a word of congratulation. She would raise her eyes and, smiling, greet the person and accept the good wishes. Then she lowered her eyes once more.

The bride-to-be on this particular evening would soon have to assume this shyness for we were warned of the coming of the bridegroom and his party—his friends and relatives (called the barat)—by a clatter and sound of music outside in the street. Suman and I ran up to the second floor to get a good look from the balcony.

It is the Hindu custom that the bridegroom walk, or preferably, ride a horse from his house to that of the bride on the eve of the wedding. But this more modern groom came in a bright yellow, flower-bedecked convertible. We could see it and the small barat procession as we looked down the street.

Leading the procession was the wedding band—two drummers and two flutists who were making a great deal of noise and only a little music but enjoying themselves immensely. Following them was the new convertible in which the groom and his closest relatives were riding. We could see that the groom was dressed in a western suit and a marvelous glittering headdress that covered all his face except his eyes and came down over his shoulders. Behind the car was a crowd of people, the groom's friends and relatives and many curious, fun-loving onlookers.

When he arrived at the door of the house the groom was greeted by some of the bride's relatives. Climbing from the car, he lifted the brightly decorated mask from his face and representatives of the two families exchanged rosewater as a symbol of good wishes. Meanwhile we and others on the balcony showered the group with flower petals.

The groom and his party then came inside to have dinner and wait for the marriage ceremony to begin. Unfortunately since it had not started by 10:30 Suman and I had to leave without seeing it. Later we found that it had not begun until midnight and had continued many hours into the night.

During my stay in India I attended several Indian weddings, Hindu and Sikh. All were rather long religious ceremonies held outdoors at the home of the bride. The couple were married after completing seven steps around a small wood fire, the ends of their clothing tied together.

One of my best friends was married in Delhi. In her bright red and gold bridal sari she looked lovely. She wore several gold bracelets and a gold chain that rested in the part of her hair. At the end of the chain was an ornament that hung down on her forehead. Her eyes had been accentuated by black marking, and tiny white dots were painted on her forehead in a simple design.

After the wedding ceremony, which took place in the early evening there was a wedding dinner at the bride's home.

Suman and I had many good times together. Yet at first she was merely someone who was nice to me, who provided me with good times when they were much needed, and who somewhat awed me by her boldness in what I had soon discovered to be a modest country. Within a couple of months she was more than that. She was a real friend and I could talk with her as I talked with my friends at home.

I remember one of January's typically beautiful days. The sky was a deep blue and the sun shone warm and bright, just warm enough so that it felt good when you put your back to it and cool enough so that you wanted to stay out of the shade unless you were wearing a heavy sweater. Suman and I and some other girls and boys had "stayed back"—stayed after school—to play hockey.

The game had finished and Suman and I were sitting in the sun resting when we saw a big dump truck go by on the road past the school. It was gaily decorated and had big posters on the sides. On each of the posters was a picture of a bullock and "Vote for Patel—Vote Congress" written in English, Hindi and Urdu. The truck was filled with people singing and shouting "Vote for Congress." Delhi State's first election was just a week away and the campaigns of each of the major Delhi parties—the Congress, Socialist, Jan Sangh and Communist—were in full swing.

I asked Suman what the bullock on the posters meant. She told me that the bullock was the symbol of the Congress party. Illiterate people could associate the symbol with the Congress party as they could associate the banyan tree with the Socialists, the diwa (oil light) with the Jan Sangh, and the wheat spike and sickle with the Communists. And they could choose the ballot box marked with the symbols of the party for which they wished to vote.

Suman asked me if we had symbols representing the

political parties in America. I told her about our Republican elephant and Democratic donkey and about our two-party system, about our elections and our political campaigns. We agreed that as far as campaigns and elections go the two countries differ little.

"But," Suman said, "India has nothing resembling your two-party system." She explained that the Congress party is the main party in India and there is no other party equal or even nearly equal to it in strength. The Socialist and the Communist parties have some strength, and the Jan Sangh a little.

The rather emotional supporters of this last party believe that India should be a purely Hindu country and that the Moslems should be forced to leave India and make their homes in Pakistan or some other Moslem state. "Besides these four parties," Suman explained, "there are other smaller ones and many independent candidates."

Suman was learning politics as I had learned them in America. In this, India's first national election, her father was an independent candidate for the Delhi State Assembly from the constituency in which he lives. "His symbol," Suman said, "is a ladder and his campaign slogan 'We want progress. Down with Congress!'" I was somewhat surprised at the slogan and told Suman I had thought that the Congress party was one of the most progressive parties in India.

"After independence we all thought it would be," Suman said, "and, indeed, it has done much for our country. But Congress has acted too slowly." Later this criticism of the Congress party was often repeated to me. Most of the people I talked to were impatient for "progress." India is in a hurry.

It was late in the afternoon when we finished talking but I felt that I knew and liked Suman much better. She was not simply the movie-going, westernized teen-ager I had previously thought her to be.

One day near the first of February, after I had been in India about three months, the girls at school decided that it was time for me to have some Indian clothes. In India clothes are made to order by men tailors called darzis. Suman suggested we go down to the cloth market and then to the shop of the darzi who usually made her clothes and have him make me a salvar and cumeez.

I agreed. I had, for some time, wanted to have a salvar and cumeez of my own. I had felt rather conspicuous in my American clothes, and a dress was not the best thing for bicycle riding. Suman and I made plans to meet in front of her home at 4:00 that afternoon.

Suman's home on Babar Road is a smallish, one-storied stucco building and she was waiting in front of it when I arrived on my bike. As we were only a short way from the market we decided to walk to the store. We walked along Babar Road, on down wide, tree-lined Barakamba Road to Connaught Circle, and around the circle to Queensway, one of New Delhi's main streets. Among the several small shops along Queensway, set up by Hindu refugees from what is now West Pakistan, there are many cloth shops and we knew that we could find something we liked there.

Soon we had bought three yards of white cotton for a salvar, two and a half yards of blue printed cotton for a cumeez, and a yard and three quarters of a light blue net-like material for a chunni. The darzi's shop was on a nearby street. We walked there, gave the tailor the cloth and told him the style I wanted. He measured me and told me to come by a week later and the clothes would be ready for me. From then on I wore Indian clothes regularly.

From the darzi's shop Suman and I went to a small stall in a bazaar nearer Suman's house where delicious-looking and, we found, delicious-tasting food was sold. We bought some indescribable spicy things and some sweets and so started a habit of which we could never break ourselves. From then on, every time I went to Suman's house we went to the little shop and filled ourselves with those delicacies.

It was not until about the first of March that I had a chance to visit Suman's home and meet her family. When I entered the house that afternoon I felt for a minute as if I were back in our usually busy home in Essex. I could hear babies crying, children laughing, the talk of grownups and the patter of many small bare feet.

The family was celebrating a young cousin's birthday and the house was overflowing with grandparents, parents, aunts and uncles, shouting children and feeding babies. There was a wonderful confusion and everyone was enjoying it, laughing and talking and having great fun. Suman introduced me to her mother and to her aunts and I entered into the confusion and was made to feel welcome.

When I left that day Suman invited me to come the next day for lunch. I had had odds and ends of Indian food and had often helped Suman and my other classmates finish their lunches at school. But not yet had I really sat down to a complete Indian meal.

When I knocked on Suman's door the next day, her small brother met me and shouted for Suman who came running, all smiles and with a grand "hi-ya" which she had recently learned from an American movie. "Hi-ya," I responded, and we sat down to talk until lunch was ready.

I asked her what members of her family were living in the house and she explained to me about the joint family system. At the head of the joint family, and at the head of Suman's family, is the grandfather and grandmother. Living with them are all their sons, married and unmarried, their married sons' wives and children, and their unmarried daughters.

"Most families in India are like this," Suman told me. "But many of the educated young people, wishing to feel independent of their parents, are making homes of their own." Suman thought, however, that the children owe much to their parents and the least they can do is look after them in their old age and respect and obey them until they die.

In Suman's household there are her grandparents (her father's mother and father), her own mother and father, her married uncle (father's brother) and his wife and children, her unmarried uncle, her unmarried aunt (father's sister), and her own two brothers and sisters.

I met almost all of them when we sat around the big dining room table to eat lunch. They greeted me shyly in English, of which they all knew at least a little, and then continued conversation among themselves in Hindustani.

Although the members of Suman's family are Hindus, like a great many Hindus, they are not vegetarians. However, like almost all Hindus, they do exclude beef from their diet. The lunch was as good as I had expected it would be. There was a highly spiced lamb curry, a delicious curry of potatoes and peas, and dhal. Dhal is a kind of mush made out of dried lentils. It is a very cheap, high-protein food and is eaten at almost every meal by people in most parts of India.

Both rice and chappaties—a round, flat, unleavened wheat bread—were served with the curries and dhal. Chappaties are a staple in almost every North Indian family and later I learned how to make them. They consist simply of whole wheat flour and enough water to make a stiff dough. The dough is kneaded well and made into small balls which are rolled out and baked for just a minute on a special iron pan on top of the fire. Other forms of unleavened bread can be made by adding oil to the dough and frying instead of baking the small discs. Rice is not eaten as much as wheat in North India. Suman's family did not have it every day.

Snowy white curds and different kinds of chutney were served with the meal and for dessert there was fruit—bananas, apples and luscious mangoes.

Suman and I spent much of the afternoon talking and then went down to the bazaar to get some of the spicy food that was so popular with us and two big handfuls—two cents worth—of deliciously sweet and juicy sugar cane.

Often after that I went to Suman's house for lunch or dinner and in those "after dinner" conversations learned much about a wonderful girl and her beautiful country.

Suman was sensitive, extremely friendly, kind and eager to learn. She was attracted by America, attracted by the America she saw in the movies, the movie magazines, and the comic books. And she tried to be as much like the American girl she found stereotyped there as she could without being what would be considered in India, with its very high moral standards, as "indecent."

She wore lipstick and rouge and eyebrow pencil and

occasionally fingernail polish and American jewelry. She preferred shoes with heels to the simple sandals which I and most other people wore. In the privacy of her home she wore dungarees (which I contributed) and chewed bubble gum. She knew the names of many, many American movie stars, danced the waltz, the fox trot and the rhumba, and said "hi-ya" and dozens of other American slang expressions.

Therefore, Suman was sometimes considered a bold, almost immodest, extravagant girl. Some even thought from what she did and wore that she cared more for America than for her own country.

But in conversations with her I learned that she was much more than that. The surface impression was not the real Suman. I came to know that Suman was as true an Indian as any of my other friends.

It was Suman who took me to the Indian wedding, who often invited me to her home to eat and take part in her family activities, in their festivals and celebrations.

It was Suman who took me to the crowded bazaars and small restaurants where I saw and was part of the teeming life of an Indian city. And it was Suman who took me to the Ram Lila where I saw India's famous epic, the Ramayana, being reenacted.

I can only hope that I helped Suman to see America as well as she helped me to understand and see her own country. I tried to tell her about the America I knew, about small town America. I described my town to her, and how the people lived and worked. I described the schools and the system of education and explained how our town and state governments are run. I told her that many girls do not wear fingernail polish and not all chew bubble gum and know the names and life histories of all the movie stars.

Still, when it came time for me to leave India, to all outward appearances Suman was more American than I, and I, who had adopted her Indian clothing, her language and many of her customs, seemed quite Indian. But down underneath, in our hearts and in our minds, Suman was an Indian and I an American.

Before I left India, Suman told me that she knew a boy

whom she liked very much and hoped to marry some day. But love-marriages are uncommon in India and I guessed that Suman would never disobey her parent's request that her husband be of the same caste as she. Suman's friend was not. So I was not surprised when I received a letter from her a while ago saying that she had become engaged, at her family's request, to a fellow of her own caste.

Suman was the best of my Delhi Public School friends, but there were others. These friendships have proved to me, as similar friendships have proved to others, that the East and West need not be strangers to each other.

FIVE

A Glimpse of the South

By December of 1951 Sally and Sam and I had seen little of India besides her two cities of Delhi, the government development project of Etawah and "places of interest" near Delhi. So we were glad when Chet made plans to visit South India in the middle of the month and we were able to take a vacation from school and go with him.

We arrived in Madras, South India's largest city, one afternoon after a six-hour plane ride from Delhi. Madras is located on India's eastern coast, washed by the waters of the Bay of Bengal. As we came nearer to the city the landscape beneath us gradually grew greener. Then Madras appeared in the far distance, a dusty grey. And beyond the greyness of the city, the great blueness of the Bay of Bengal stretched farther than we could see, somewhere merging with the blue of the sky. In the harbor dozens of tankers, freighters, coastal passenger steamers and small sailing craft lay at anchor, basking in the sun, or hurried busily here and there.

As we circled nearer to the ground the details of lovely little palm trees and rice fields gradually emerged and we knew that we were in the South.

We stayed in Madras only a day. During that time we learned a few words of Tamil, the sweet-sounding language of most South Indians. Like two of the three other main languages of South India, Telegu and Kanarese, Tamil is completely unrelated to Sanskrit or its derivative languages.

Hindustani is as foreign to the South Indian as English, and its adoption as the national language has not been warmly approved in the South. Many feel that it is wrong to give up English as the *lingua franca* of India now that it is such a widely spoken language throughout the world.

Beginning at 6:30 in the morning, we spent our day in Madras visiting many institutions and organizations. Our last visit was to a recreation and health center which resembled the settlement houses in this country. The center provided complete health and recreational services for about 300 families in the neighborhood. Children could spend the day there, go to school, take part in organized recreation and receive medical care.

This organization and most of the others we visited were founded for the express purpose of helping a segment of India's people reach a higher standard of living. Most of the people working in these organizations and institutions seemed to have a great hopefulness and feeling of pride in their efforts. They were proud of their work, probably because they believed, as I believe, that the greatest bit one can do, even if it is small, when combined with the tiny successes of other people, will amount to a big and important success. Later we found these same hopeful attitudes in many parts of India.

We left Madras early the next morning by car for the city of Bangalore, 250 miles to the west. Early in the afternoon, soon after crossing from Madras state into the state of Mysore, we stopped at the town of Kolar. Here we were garlanded and welcomed by a Christian missionary group from America active in public health and literacy work in the Kolar area. This was the first time I had come in contact with American missionaries and I was impressed with the work they were doing.

I had heard so often of another kind of missionary, the missionary whose only objective is to convert the Indian people with whom he is working to Christianity. Therefore I was happy to meet the Kolar missionaries and learn that all missionaries are not bent only on conversion as I had understood.

Later I came to know other missionaries who channel their energies into secular activities. I learned of groups all over India who are working as selflessly and as "Christian-like" as those in Kolar. The majority of the missionaries in India are Roman Catholic. Most of the remaining are either Episcopalian or Methodist.

As we had come closer to Kolar, the scenery had gradually grown more barren, and boulder-covered hills rose from the plain. Here the crops of rice and milo and millet were thirsting for water.

In the greener, less barren places, we passed small villages. Occasionally we saw a small house made of stone or brick, rather conspicuous among the common mud structures, thatched with palm roofs. On the edge of many of the villages was a beautifully carved stone Hindu temple. There were signs also of Christianity and Mohammedanism.

Beside the road, lovely banyan trees spread over long distances. Their branches grew to amazing lengths, supported by other branches which had grown downward and become rooted in the ground.

We reached Bangalore in the evening and left early the next morning, headed southwestward for the city of Mysore where we stopped to visit the Maharaja of Mysore's palace. The Maharaja was not at home but we were shown through the palace by some of his aides. I was astounded by it as I had been by the Taj Mahal Hotel in Bombay, astounded and angered at the contrast it presented with the poverty-stricken streets through which we had come.

There was gold and silver and marble, glass furniture, glittering showrooms and halls full of stuffed animals. It was like the legendary palaces I had heard about in fairy tales as a child, palaces which I had not thought really existed.

When we left that world of fantasy, on a street near the palace, we were stopped by a policeman and informed that we would have to take a detour, that His Highness was coming and the street must be cleared. My heart rebelled and I wondered if this rebellion was the result of my upbringing as an American or whether the man on the Mysore street felt similarly. I wondered also how His Highness felt at having his former subjects pushed from his path. Perhaps they have both known nothing different.

Since the independence of the country, the political power of such hereditary maharajas has dwindled to almost nothing. Some have been elected to office and are dedicating their lives to the building of the New India. Others still lead luxurious lives on the money given to them by the Indian government when their princely powers were removed.

From Mysore we headed south towards Ootacamund, a town high in the Nilgiris Hills, a part of the Western Ghat Mountains. As we climbed higher the vegetation gradually became more dense. Soon we were surrounded by gorgeous green forest, a forest of frail, spindly bamboo trees, tall and stately teak, and oil-bearing graceful eucalyptus. I remember it now as the most beautiful part of India that I visited during my stay there. I had missed this green, woodsy, hilly type of country so much in dry, flat Delhi.

As we wound higher and higher, almost coming to a stop at hairpin curves, it grew colder. We passed plantations of little tea bushes, systematically terraced rice fields, and acres of government owned cinchona trees, raised for the quinine in their bark.

We spent the following day, a Sunday, at Ootacamund, basking in the luxuriant greenness. It was only a little more than a week until Christmas. That night Sally and I and a South Indian Christian, who was travelling with us, went to a pre-Christmas service in a small church perched on a hill overlooking the town market place. The church, built in the early 1800's, was small and simple. By the time we arrived it was already crowded with people, from stooping grandparents to tiny blanket-bundled babies, jacketed, fur-capped fathers and women wrapped in warm woolen shawls.

The simplicity of the church and the service was lovely.

A plain wooden cross, tall white candles and boughs of greenery adorned the altar. The service, conducted both in Tamil and in English, consisted mainly of carol singing.

The Tamil carols were more lively and spirited than the ones usually sung in America, but they were sung seriously and with meaning.

In travelling to Ootacamund, we had come up the northern side of the mountains. Two days later when we left, we drove down the southern side, headed for the town of Cochin in the coastal state of Travancore-Cochin. Our road gradually grew less curvy and finally became flat and straight at the foot of the mountains. Tall areca palms and fields of rice, cotton and cashew, crops typical of the hot, wet country into which we had descended, grew on either side of the road.

We knew it was in South India that we would be able to see the elephants which we, while still in America, had thought were common all over India. That day, on our way from Ootacamund to Cochin we saw our first elephant, a wild one.

Near a small village two miles off the main road a baby elephant had been caught in a trap which had been dug and concealed for that purpose. The small dirt road through the woods to the village was deeply rutted and therefore impassable by our car. We accepted the offer of a kindly bullock-cart driver with two, slow-plodding bullocks to take us and bring us back.

There was a small crowd around the pit watching the little elephant (if a baby elephant can be called little) struggling pathetically into exhaustion. Wild elephants are very destructive to the farmers' crops. Tame and trained they are extremely useful, as we saw later in the day when we passed an occasional elephant at work, usually dragging branches or logs.

As we came nearer to the coast the soil grew more sandy and our road passed over many small streams, canals and other waterways. At one point we and our car were poled across a shallow but wide and swiftly flowing river on a ferry made simply of a wooden platform resting on two long dugouts.

It was dusk when we arrived at the river and dark by

the time we finally reached the other side. The moon was just rising over the trees on the farther bank and the light was reflected in a ripply sort of way in the water. There was a lovely peaceful quietness interrupted only by the distant clamoring of a multitude of peep-frogs and the quiet murmur of men's voices at a small tea shop at the side of the road where we waited our turn at the ferry.

We left Cochin early the next morning for Cape Comorin, at the very tip of India. It was a beautiful and lush land that we passed through that day and unlike any part of India I had seen so far. At first glance Travancore-Cochin seemed prosperous, content and peaceful. The land was lovely in its natural scenery—the tall, graceful coconut palms silhouetted against the blueness of the sky, the dense greenery, the white sand of the endless beach, the calm blue-greenness of the great ocean that stretched all the way to Africa, and the small thatch-roofed village homes which extended along the coast in a continuous, almost uninterrupted line, blending with the earth and the trees.

The land was rich too, in its plentiful natural growth, in the coconut palms which provided almost all the necessities of life, in its abundant rainfall and temperate climate.

But the beauty and the richness were deceiving. Under their false front lay India's worst poverty, terrible over-population, a strangling system of land ownership and the violence of the Communists who seem drawn inevitably to such regions.

The majority of the villagers of that coastal area are almost entirely dependent on the coconut palms that grow so abundantly around them. They waste no part of the big tree.

The coconuts which we in America can buy in the store originally have a green, fiber-lined husk. Before the coconut comes to us, laborers remove this shell which, when scraped clean of the fiber, is valuable for fuel and fertilizer. The villagers use the fiber in making rope and weaving mats and baskets.

Inside the husk is the seed which contains what we know as coconut "meat." This meat is often eaten as is or it is dried and shredded for export or pressed to extract the coconut oil. The white coconut milk is a wonderful thirst-quenching drink.

Everywhere we saw parts of the coconut palm in one form or another. Most of the roofs of the small homes were thatched with the broad coconut palm leaves, and mats and baskets were woven of leaf strips or made of coir, the fibrous lining of the coconut husks.

Huge baskets and carts and, near the sea and in the canals, boats were filled with the green husks. Other baskets were piled high with the fibrous lining. And in many places, spread out on mats at the side of the road, the coconut meat was drying in the warm sun.

The majority of the people in the area work in various phases of the coconut production and industry. But they are poorly paid by rich and powerful landlords over whom they have little or no control. It is no wonder that they are discontent and are easily led to violence.

Land reform was an important issue in the political campaign, signs of which we saw everywhere. In India's first democratic election, in 1951, each province had a different date of voting. Travancore-Cochin's was to come soon after we left. Posters and stickers, flags, election cars and carts, rallies, meetings and parades advertised candidates and parties. As often as the sober green, red and white of Nehru and the Congress party, we saw the bright violent red of the United Front of Communist and left wing parties. In one village we passed a short parade of excited men carrying red flags and shouting in unison and in the regional language, "Vote for the Communist party."

Later, back in Delhi after the election returns had come in, I learned that the Communists had failed to win a majority of seats in the state government. In 1954 new elections were held and we were happy to hear that the Communist strength seemed to be gradually lessening.

We reached Cape Comorin in the evening. Here, at the very foot of India, I met a little girl I think I shall long remember. Her name was Mary and she looked about ten years old. We found her on the beach where she approached us, determined to sell us some pretty shell necklaces which she had made. When we had satisfied her she at once removed her mask of seriousness and her business-like attitude, stuffed her remaining wares in her pocket and became a gay child of the sea and the sand. As we walked up the beach she ran ahead of us, playing an endless game with the waves which tried in vain to catch her toes. With her imaginative help Sally, Sam and I built the most elaborate sand castle.

When we left, Mary was on the deserted beach where we had found her. She was as wild as the wind, as playful as the waves of the sea and as lovely as the sand and the pretty shells, her playmates.

Standing on the beach at Cape Comorin, at the very tip of the Indian peninsula, I felt very alone and separate. At my feet the great grey-blue waters of the Arabian Sea, the Bay of Bengal and the Indian Ocean came together and stretched farther southward than the eye could see. Somehow I felt that I was being pushed into this great expanse of sea, wind, sky and lovely orange sunsets before me. Behind me, pushing, was the teeming humanity of the Indian peninsula.

Standing there alone, I thought of the universe as divided into two very different parts. One was symbolized for me by the great expanse of sea, wind and sky that stretched in front of me. This I called the Greatness of Nature. It was beautiful, but impersonal and lonely.

The other component of the universe was symbolized for me by the crowded population of India behind me. This component was the one human race, Humanity. It was personal, warm and friendly, yet often overpowering and incomprehensible, artificially divided into intricate and conflicting groups and further divided into individual personalities.

We left South India the next day, from the city of Trivandrum, fifty miles up the western coast. Previously I had divided the sub-continent into two very general halves—North and South India. Before I had come to the South I had begun to love India as represented by Delhi and the generally dry and colorful northern half. Now, after my two weeks in the green, wet, sober country of South India, I loved India the more and felt more justified in saying I loved India.

SIX

Sevagram, Gandhi's Village

IN THE HEART of India, in her central province of Madhya Pradesh, there lies a small but tremendously important village. Its name, Sevagram, means "service village."

The name Sevagram and the importance of the little village are new. The village itself is old and was like any small Indian village until the spring of 1935, when a man revered throughout India, Mahatma Gandhi, went there to make his home.

On the edge of the village Gandhiji set up an ashram, a shelter, a place where he and others could live according to Gandhian principles. His chief purpose in creating this ashram at Sevagram was to prove that a decent society could be developed even in India's most backward village. The main step in the realization of this aim was the creation, by Gandhi and two of his disciples, Aryanayakam and his wife Asha Devi, of a system of education—New Education or Nai Talim—which was finally put into practice in schools at Sevagram. Gandhi, believing that "there is nothing in life, however small, which is not the concern of education," called this an "education for life."

Steb, who is especially interested in education and public health work, wanted very much to visit Sevagram. So one evening in the middle of January, 1952, she, Sally, Sam and I boarded a southbound train in the Delhi Railway Station and settled ourselves comfortably in a small second-class compartment. Soon our train was chugging slowly out of the station and then, gaining speed, it left the city behind and rushed into the darkness. We expected to arrive in Wardha, a small depot about five miles from Sevagram, the next night.

Our compartment had two leather-cushioned seats and two berths that let down from the wall, making it possible to sleep four. Like all Indian train compartments, it stretched across the entire car. It had two doors, one on either side, and there were two barred windows on each side which could be opened. On the ceiling was an electric light and a fan. The compartment was in no way connected with adjacent compartments and thus it was impossible to go in or out except when the train was standing in the station.

That night we were the only ones in the compartment and we had a comfortable sleep, lulled by the click clack of the wheels on the rails. However our sleep was frequently disturbed by the cries of the vendors when we stopped in the stations. Cries of "Narangi, narangi, acche acche narangi" (oranges, good oranges), "garm dudh, garrrrrm dudh" (hot milk), "dalsev, dalsev wala" (dalsev is something like potato sticks, wala means seller of), "chae, chae, garm chae" (hot tea) rang out at intervals during the night. By the time I left India, these sounds were no more than a pleasant background to my dreams when I travelled by train, but that night they were strange and new and they awakened us.

Sometimes a beggar joined his cry with that of the vendors. Once a spry looking child poked his head in at the window whining, "Do paisa do, memsahib. Man nahin hain, memsahib. Bhuka hain." "Give me two pice, memsahib. My mother is dead. I am hungry," he implored us. But he looked well fed and healthy so we feigned sleep. It was not so easy to turn our backs on other deformed, crippled or pitifully thin beggars.

During the next day we got out at almost all of the frequent, perhaps hourly, stops, to get a drink of water, to buy some fruit or merely to stretch our legs. We walked up and down along the train and inspected the first-, inter-class and third-class compartments.

The first-class compartments looked little different from our second-class one. They were planned to seat fewer people and perhaps the seats were softer. The first-class ticket cost almost twice at much as our second-class one and few people could really afford it. Why a person ever went first class I cannot imagine unless it was a matter of prestige.

The inter-class compartments were a little bigger than

the second-class ones and were meant to hold many more people; the bench seats were narrower and had just a thin layer of leather cushion on them. The third-class compartments were almost always terribly crowded and had no cushions on the narrow benches. Our second-class tickets from Delhi to Wardha had cost about sixty rupees or approximately twelve dollars each. A third-class ticket probably cost not more than twenty rupees or four dollars.

Later, when I travelled alone, I always went third class. It was there that I met Indians of all walks of life, was able to talk with them, to share their food and play with their children.

How different these third-class compartment train rides, and even the second-class compartment ride to Sevagram, were from our ride to the country of Nepal a month later in two super first-class train compartments—and how differently I felt. The elaborateness of our travel to Nepal was embarrassing to me and I wished that elaborateness and wealth were not traditionally synonymous with diplomacy and government officials.

I am sure that the people who watched us with such curiosity in the stations through which we passed on our way to Nepal acted differently before men whom they considered to be of superior rank than they acted with their own friends and equals. Because of this I wished that my parents and the other Embassy people who were with us could somehow disguise themselves and meet those people as equals.

We could learn factually of these people. We could greet each other and smile together. Our meeting would be friendly, but formal. I do not believe that you can have a truly informal, close relationship with a person or his family or his village people on this basis. It seems to me that you must be accepted by the person or the group, either for what you are, which unfortunately usually takes time, or for your identification with the person or group, in action, speech and dress. My hope is that the people of the world may soon have the opportunity and the desire to know each other on the basis of accepting others for what each is, each realizing that he is really little different from any other and that the differences that do exist need not stand in the way of friendship.

There was another side to the elaborate first-class ride to Nepal that bothered me, as I know similar rides bothered others. Gandhi once said, "We should be ashamed of resting or having a square meal so long as there is one able-bodied man or woman without work or food." So Gandhi ate only a minimum of food and rested only as a necessity, devoting the remainder of his time to helping make it possible that every man and woman might have work and food.

I do not believe, as Gandhi did, that one should feel ashamed to take food and rest because others are "without work or food." But I do believe that there is such a thing as too much food, too much rest and too much display of wealth. There is a point at which one can be comfortable and every human being deserves this comfort—employment, a secure home, decent food and as much education as one desires and can absorb. To go beyond this into luxury, it seems to me, is unnecessary and wrong.

So I was sorry that our travel to Nepal had to be so elaborate. But according to protocol, on that gala occasion such elaborateness was expected of us. How much more comfortable—mentally if not physically—was our travel to Sevagram.

The stations, like the trains, were crowded. Coolies carrying small metal trunks or heavy boxes or baskets on their heads rushed up and down the platform looking in the train windows for empty seats. Whole families trailed after them. Vendors pushed their way among the crowd on the platform, maneuvering small carts or carefully balancing baskets filled with the wares they frequently and very loudly publicized. A man passed from window to window of the train filling the brass tankards and clay jugs of the passengers with drinking water, unavailable in the compartments.

Waits for trains were often long and families sat on the edge of the platform eating or resting. People clustered round the water tap, drinking water and bathing. Men washed by pouring water over themselves from their own jar-like brass lotas. Skillfully they changed to clean dhotis, washed the dhotis they had had on and spread them out to dry in the hot sun.

We reached Wardha in the evening, after a somewhat dirty but pleasant trip. A tall man, dressed in white homespun cotton, came up to us at once, greeted us and introduced himself as Aryanayakam. We knew him to be, with his wife Asha Devi (later one of my mother's and father's best friends), the director of the Basic Education School at Sevagram, and one of Gandhiji's closest associates.

As we chugged along the dusty road in an old car to the ashram (I felt somehow as if I should be walking), our host pointed out the dairy, the hospital and the library, all of which we would visit in the morning. We arrived at the ashram just in time to join the rest of the community for evening prayers.

We sat down quietly on the ground under the dim starlit sky, on the edge of the gathering. The prayers were sung or chanted in Marathi and Hindustani so we could not understand them. But by the phrasing I thought I recognized the Lord's Prayer. Later we learned that the prayers we heard that night were prayers of every religion and the Lord's Prayer had been one of them. High caste and untouchable Hindus, Mohammedans and Christians gathered together, praised God in the words of the Koran, the Bible and the Bhagavad-Gita. It was quiet there, and peaceful.

After the prayer meeting our host, Mr. Aryanayakam, and his daughter Mitu, who was my age, took us to visit the small mud hut in which Gandhiji lived when he came to Sevagram on his "holidays" from prison. His few and simple belongings were just as he had left them.

To many Indians the hut is almost sacred, and standing in the one small room no one spoke in more than a whisper. Indeed, I did not feel like speaking.

A few hundred yards away from Gandhi's hut was the simple mud and bamboo guest house where we were to stay. We went there and had an Indian supper made almost completely of produce grown in the ashram garden. The food was simple and very moderately spiced, but good—rice, chappaties, vegetable curry and dhal, and rice pudding for dessert.

One of Gandhiji's dreams was that one day each Indian village might be self-sufficient. He once said: "My idea in village swaraj (self-government) is that it is a complete republic, independent of its neighbors for its own vital wants, and yet inter-dependent for many others in which dependence is a necessity. Thus every village's first concern will be to grow its own food crops and cotton for cloth. It should have a reserve for its cattle, recreation and playground for adults and children. The village will maintain a village theater, school and public hall. . . . Education will be compulsory up to the final basic course. As far as possible every activity will be conducted on the co-operative basis." Sevagram was trying to prove that this goal could someday be reached everywhere in India.

There were no servants at Sevagram. It was Aryanaya-kam's daughter, Mitu, and her friends who prepared our food. I talked with Mitu, who had been educated at the college at Sevagram, before we went to bed. Unlike most of her friends, she knew English. She told me how surprised everyone was that we had brought no servants with us and that we carried only a small knapsack each for our extra clothing (we would stay only two days). I was surprised that she was surprised.

In America, I said, few people have servants. And because we don't have servants, we take only what is necessary when we travel. We were Americans, and I did not think that this or anything else gave us a right to act extravagantly. I said that as Americans I felt we should act as Americans do at home, unless in so doing our actions conflicted with Indian customs.

Mitu agreed that it would have been unnatural for us to bring servants. She told me that usually when "important" persons came they brought their own servants and much luggage. I wondered if Mitu and the other members of the community felt sorry, as I did, for those persons in their dependence on complicated living.

We slept on low, table-like, mosquito-netted, quilt-covered beds. It was a beautiful night.

Sevagram village had been picked as the cite for Gandhiji's ashram according to his specific directions—the poorest village in the poorest part of India. One of his requirements was that there be no electricity until it became cheaper and available even to the poorest villager. The people who were still awake were quietly doing their tasks with the help of softly-burning kerosene lanterns.

The first light of dawn was just appearing when someone called us softly. We dressed and were ready for breakfast in the community eating room by 6:30. But we were comparative sleepyheads. Some of the earliest risers had been to a prayer meeting at 4:30. The whole ashram had been awake by 5:30 and busy at morning tasks, mainly breakfast preparation, since then.

The room was already filled with school and college students and their teachers—of all castes and creeds—sitting in rows on the earthen floor. We too sat down and were supplied with an empty copper bowl. Soon a student brigade entered, carrying big buckets of porridge and pitchers of hot milk. When everyone was served, a short prayer was said and a blessing sung.

As each finished eating, he took his bowl and cup outside and scrubbed them clean with ashes and water. Then the ashram students, divided into pre-arranged groups, did small jobs such as washing the kitchen pots and pans, cleaning the grounds, drawing water from the well and so on.

The rest of the student's day was spent in class and farm work. (Each student averaged two hours of farm work a day.) In his leisure time he could do as he pleased —study, wash clothing or spin. Spinning was a favorite pastime. Besides being a useful work, it was restful and provided an opportunity to think and meditate.

After breakfast, when the dew was still on the ground, we walked through the fields and saw the healthy crops of vegetables, maize, corn and cotton, and the groves of banana, orange and papaya. Most of these crops had never before been grown by the villagers in the area. When Gandhiji first arrived at the village, almost the only crops in the region were cotton and castor beans.

We met a college student driving two well-fed bullocks around a well, pulling up bucket after bucket of clear water on an endless chain. The water flowed steadily into small irrigation ditches which crisscrossed the garden where his classmates were working. It is a new thing in India to see college students getting their hands dirty, working in the sun doing farm work. But that is one of the most important parts of the education of a Sevagram student.

We walked back through the fields to the poultry yard and dairy. These were just one step ahead of the simplest village poultry farm and dairy but were clean and well ventilated. Everything was simple and within the average villager's understanding. But because the poultry and cattle were healthy and well fed, the hens were producing more eggs and the cows giving more milk than the village people had at first thought possible. Small changes had made great improvements.

From the dairy we visited the small ashram library. The librarian was an old man, a German from South Africa. His library contained perhaps only a few hundred books but they were written in many languages and on many subjects.

We then visited the Pre-Basic school for children up to seven years of age. A young man, the teacher, met us and showed us through the small school. Most of the children we saw were ginning, carding or spinning the cotton which they had grown and recently picked. Some of them were singing at their work. They looked happy, responsive and clean.

The teacher explained that most of the children come in from the village of Sevagram for the day. Raising cotton, he told us, was not merely a craft. The small students learned general science as they grew and picked the cotton, and arithmetic as they figured how much they had grown and how much work they had done. They learned geography as they discussed other places in the world where cotton was grown and where the cotton they had grown might finally go, and social studies as they talked of the government and people of those countries.

This is Gandhiji's basic education in practice and in some ways it is like the "learning by doing" approach of the public schools which I attended in America. The basic education curriculum is being adopted in the great majority of schools growing up in India.

Later in the afternoon we visited the area's hospital a mile or two away from the ashram. This hospital serves about seventy-five villagers in the area surrounding Sevagram. Besides acting as a village medical research center, it also gives training to student teachers of the basic education department to enable them to run school dispensaries in villages where no other medical aid is available.

From Sevagram we drove into the town of Wardha, to the All-India Village Industries Association which Gandhiji also started. Here craftsmen from many parts of India were being trained in paper-making, pottery, soap-making, oil pressing and bee keeping, all done without complex machinery.

The All-India Village Industries Association building is open to visitors with the hope that interest in such industries may be spread. The people running this organization believe, as Gandhiji did, that if village people would develop simple village industries, plant resources now going to waste could be made use of and farmers, who are forced to be idle when there is no work in the fields, could be kept busy and wage-earning the year round.

That night before I went to sleep soon after the nightly prayer meeting, I felt more strongly than before the peacefulness around me, the quiet and the happiness. I thought how revolutionary—peacefully revolutionary— was Sevagram's community way of living, of working, studying and playing. I understood why, to so many, Sevagram represents India's hope for the future, her leader in the country's great social revolution. Now I regarded Sevagram as more than a village of service. It is a village of peace and of hope.

Gandhi once said, "When our villages are fully developed there will be no dearth in them of men with a high degree of skill and artistic talent. There will be village poets, village artists, village architects, linguists and research workers. In short, there will be nothing in life worth having which will not be had in the villages. Today the villages of India are dung heaps. Tomorrow they will be like tiny gardens of Eden where dwell highly intelligent folk whom no one can deceive or exploit."

Gandhi was an idealist, but a deeply practical one, and if an India of "tiny gardens of Eden" ever does come into existence, Sevagram's forceful example of community living and development, and the system of New Education as exemplified in the schools at Sevagram, will be an important step in its creation.

Soon after breakfast the next morning we said goodbye to our friends and to Sevagram. We were especially sorry to leave Mr. Aryanayakam. We felt that his was the kind of faith necessary to guide India through the next and immensely important few years of her development.

We left Sevagram for the city of Nagpur where we were to get a plane for New Delhi. On the way we stopped at the small ashram of Vinoba Bhave. The ashram itself was not especially impressive, but Vinobaji has achieved considerable prominence. He worked closely with Gandhi in the struggle for independence and is probably, except for Prime Minister Nehru, the person best known to the Indian people today.

In 1951, Vinoba began a movement which he called the Bhoodan-yagna, or the Land Gift Movement. Vinoba, like so many others, believes that land reform and land redistribution is a very important part of India's growth as a new nation and feels that, due to landowner influence in the legislatures, the government is working too slowly on this issue.

So, walking from one village to another, from one province of India to another, he asks those who have land to share it with those who have none. To those who have land he says: "I have come to loot you with love. . . . Many of India's people are landless. If one of you has five sons and a sixth is born to him, you will divide your property into six parts instead of five. I am asking for one-sixth of India's soil on behalf of the landless. Consider me as your sixth son."

The results of this simple appeal have been remarkable. Since he began his campaign Vinoba has received more than four million acres of land which are being distributed as quickly as possible to formerly landless peasants.

At school the next day I wondered what good it was for Suman and my other friends at Delhi Public School to be studying such subjects as geometry and English literature if they wished to be of the greatest service to their country in this stage of its development. With the education they were getting they would, upon graduation, either take a comfortable white collar office job or join the crowd of unemployed who were seeking such jobs.

I realized while at Sevagram that the real need for India's young men and women is in the villages. A Delhi Public School education provides no preparation for plowing, public health work or a village literacy campaign. What a difference a basic education would have meant to my citified, "sophisticated" friends.

When I told these thoughts to Suman, I was somewhat scolded for them. "You do not understand," she said. "Even if I wanted to, and once or twice I have felt that I would like to, it would not be a simple matter to skip off to Sevagram, go through their Post Basic college and settle down in some tiny village.

"Think what my parents would say. They would never allow it. If I disobeyed them and ran away they would be heart-broken and greatly saddened to think that one of their daughters whom they had so carefully and lovingly brought up, had lost all respect for her parents and had so grossly disobeyed them.

"It would be hard too, for me, to give up the little luxuries—the silk saries, my jewelry, my lipstick and my movie-going—now so much a part of my life."

Suman's reply, I realized, was in a sense understandable. Caste restrictions, ideas about the degradation of manual labor and the custom of early, intra-caste marriages, were firmly imbedded in her way of life and that of others like her.

While discussing this question with Suman, I thought of a training center for village workers that we had visited soon after we came to India. (There are now more than forty such centers throughout the country.) In this training center, as at Sevagram, the workers were encouraged to ally themselves as closely as possible with the villagers, to regard themselves as villagers and learn to respect the customs, traditions and way of life of the village people.

I tried to imagine Suman in such a position. Her job would be to convince the farmer's wife and the only way she could be successful would be to demonstrate her improved methods. She would have to work side by side with the village women.

This would mean not only a complete abandonment of her "little luxuries," but would involve working in the hot sun and getting her hands dirty. But for centuries the people of her class have looked upon such labor as degrading, beneath their dignity. No, even if Suman wanted to, her parents would never allow her to work in the villages. And such, I realized, was the attitude of many Indian parents, especially those who lived in the cities.

Nevertheless, I realized too that the number of parents who are allowing their sons and daughters to cross these lines of caste and custom is daily increasing. Many of these parents have been influenced by Gandhi and Gandhian ideals. Others have been influenced by the growing demand of young people to break away from the traditional ties of their caste and the joint family system. And the fact that the Indian government has taken a firm stand against caste, and has prohibited discrimination on the basis of caste by employers, has undoubtedly had a great deal of influence upon many Indians.

Most of India's college graduates, however, are caught between the old India of their parents and this new India of the Five Year Plan. Many graduate from college with a feeling of insecurity, with a sense of not belonging either to the new or the old. The step to Communism is a short one for many such frustrated individuals. Happily many of them soon become disillusioned and break away.

Suman's grandmother and mother would not have dreamed of doing village work. Suman had thought of it. Perhaps her child, with but mild disapproval, may work in the villages.

I believe the time is not far off when the 600,000 villages will no longer be thought of as remote poverty-

stricken mud holes, but as the next door neighbors of
the cities and the very most important centers of Indian
life.

SEVEN

Children with Problems

Not many months went by before I began to feel dis-
satisfied with my life as a Delhi Public School student.
By that time I had seen other parts of India besides New
Delhi and knew that her broad, tree-lined streets and
large, elaborate houses belonged more to a city of Europe
than to a city of India.

I had visited Nepal, that new and uncertain democracy,
and Sevagram, that peaceful village island, where, I think,
my dissatisfaction was really born. I had come to know
many of the Indian and Nepali people and had learned
some of their problems. I had seen the suffering of others
whom I did not know, and I knew they should not have
to suffer.

There was, I realized, much to be done and too few
willing to do it. And so I became determined to do my
share, even though I knew that, as a fifteen-year-old, what
I could do would be small.

Since my days in grammar school I had been interested
in nursing work. So through an Englishwoman my mother
knew who had worked in Delhi hospitals, I was able, in
early March of 1952, to get a volunteer job in the children's ward of Irwin Hospital, one of Delhi's government-
supported hospitals.

The first day the nurse in charge of the ward wrote out
a pass for me but I never had to use it. I came and went
as I liked. At first, in March and April when school was
still in session, I worked from about 4:30 until 7:00 or
later, often until 8:00 or 8:30. Because I loved the work,
it was more often a case of my *having* to go home rather

than wanting to go. In May, when school closed for the summer, I worked all afternoon—sometimes as late as seven o'clock. I went every day and always came home feeling tired but happy. When I was with the children I could forget my own small problems.

The ward was a long wing of the hospital with an open porch all along one side, making the room fairly light and airy. There were about forty beds in two rows on either side of the ward. Sometimes there were more patients than beds and once as many as fifteen mattresses were put on the floor for the less serious cases. I was glad that the hospital had not set such high standards for itself that it refused to accept the extra patients.

My particular ward was for children with non-contagious ailments, most of which required surgery. There were children with inflamed tonsils, bad burns, compound fractures, and infections. Many were victims of street accidents. One of my favorite little girls had a curable blindness and I watched with great excitement as she grew better. She was lonesome in her blindness and each day I lifted her from her crib and carried her as I went around the ward visiting the other children.

The children were hungry for any non-medical attention I could give them. There were far too few nurses and the kind of thing I was able to do had usually been left undone.

Except when they had taken ether for an operation, I gave the children water, which was in great demand in the hot weather. As weeks went on, they taught me enough Hindustani so that I could sit and talk with those who felt able. Sometimes the nurses asked me to help them by holding a child for one of his daily penicillin injections or by comforting another while he was being bandaged. When I stayed during their mealtime I helped feed those unable to feed themselves.

But it was my association with the toy cupboard that the children liked best. The nurse in charge had given me a big key which opened a cupboard on the porch, filled with things to play with—balls and games, stuffed dolls, toy cars, drums, puzzles, crayons, and paints, scrap books and story books.

The drums created a real problem. They were new and brightly decorated and, of all the toys, were in greatest demand. There were only three and the children were constantly squabbling among themselves to get one. But the noise was the worst of it. Asking little people to beat quietly was, I found, useless. So one afternoon the drums disappeared mysteriously from the ward!

Each day when I came into the ward I went first to get the big key and was met by five or six of those children who could walk around. I looked forward so much to their greeting and to hear them shout, "Bahenji aee hain, Bahenji aee hain," "Sister has come, Sister has come." They made sure that the first thing I did each day was to open the toy cupboard.

To each of the bedridden children I took a toy, said "namaste," and talked for a while. Sometimes one of the children wanted to hear a story and after seeing that all the other children had something to play with, I would come back to his bed and read to him and the others who gathered round.

For the first few weeks I couldn't say much to them in Hindustani, the only language most of them knew. But I could read it. I had learned the Deva Nagri alphabet at school and even though I could not always understand what I read, the children understood and enjoyed my reading to them. One of their favorite stories was *Lal Murgi*, the story of the little red hen that so many American children are familiar with.

But every day my Hindustani vocabulary increased. Each day I tried to pick out of conversations two or three words that I didn't know so that when I got home I could ask Shakur their meaning. By the time I left the hospital my Hindustani was a child's language, filled with slang and wrong verb forms, but it was a bridge between myself and the children and that was what was important.

I clearly remember one of my language mix-ups. A ten-year-old boy had a painful fracture in his leg and therefore could not move from the bed. He liked me to stay by him and talk and sometimes play games. One gloomy, cloudy day, I gave him some paints and a coloring book.

"Barush hai?" he asked me.

"No," I said, "it is not raining." ("Barish" means rain.) "But it might any minute."

"Nahin, Bahenji," he said. "Barush, barush, opkepas barush hai?" And only then I realized that he was asking me, in plain English, for the paint brush which I had left in the cupboard and forgotten to give him!

It was a sad moment when I left in the evening and had to put the toys away, usually just before the visiting hour. But the children knew that their parents would be coming soon and I consoled them with that thought. Most of the parents and friends who came during the visiting hour were poor and few were able to pay for their child's hospital care. But they loved the children and brought sweets and fruit and all kinds of little toys. Many of the parents lived far from the hospital and, undoubtedly, there were other children at home. But each day nearly every child had a visitor.

Most of the children stayed in the hospital at least a week. Within a couple of days I would learn the name of a newcomer and he would learn that I was the bahenji that came every day to help and play with the children. Then we became good friends and if he was one of those who was to have an operation he would know that I, a friend, would be in the ward when he got back.

When the children were on their feet they were as mischievous as little devils, and I had my hands full trying to keep them both quiet and happy. I became really attached to those who stayed at the hospital more than a week or so, and although there were always others to take their places, I missed each litle individual when he went home.

The few nurses who were in the ward were usually busy and changed every two weeks, so I did not get to know any of them well. Some, it seemed to me, had become nurses, not out of a sense of social service, but simply to support themselves until their marriage. Not all of them were sympathetic with the children. Almost all of the nurses and many of the doctors had been trained in Delhi. Several of the doctors had taken their training in England; a few had trained in the United States.

I remember some of those children so clearly. There was Kasturi, who had spilled boiling water on herself and was badly burned from the waist down. She lived in a small mud home near the hospital, on the road to the spot where some of Gandhi's ashes are buried, a place revered throughout India. Her father and uncles, she said, were laborers working on one of the many buildings going up in the neighborhood. I always looked forward to seeing her.

And there was the little boy with an infected foot whom the nurses had nicknamed Chupa, meaning the silent one. Like most of the children there was little difference between him and any American child.

He was the most affectionate of all the children and whenever I went past his crib he would reach his arms up for me to take him out. The little one would not play with me or the other children but loved me to carry him wherever I went. The nurses said that he couldn't talk. Indeed, I never heard him, except one hot day, while getting some ice water for another child, I rubbed a piece of ice against his leg. He smiled one of his few smiles and said "tanda"—cold. After that I knew that he could talk and felt that perhaps being in an unfamiliar place among strangers had just made him too frightened to speak.

I remember Mohan, too, who had a broken collarbone. He had to lie flat on his back, his neck in an uncomfortable cast. He used to tease me about the way I mixed up my Hindustani and like so many others, he kidded me about my freckles.

The child I remember best is little lame-legged Ram Chand. This wonderful little twelve-year-old was in the hospital for at least a month during the summer. Then, three months later, he was back again. I knew him the longest of all the children. Others would come and go but he would stay. He knew all the orderlies, the doctors and the nurses, and limping around the ward, he came to know all the other children. He was mischievous without ever being mean.

The week before I left the hospital he had his operation and when I came in in the afternoon he lay very still and sick on his bed, his lame leg in a big plaster cast. He smiled at me and asked me to sit by his bed for a while and talk. When I left the hospital for good he was still in his cast, quiet and brave and lonely. His parents lived in a small village outside of Delhi and were rarely able to come and see him.

After two months at college, I came back to the hospital for a month. The children's ward had been moved to a new building. This ward was much airier and cheerier. The walls were painted pretty pastel colors, the lights were soft but bright and each child had a little cupboard in which he could put his things.

This ward was nearer the street and vendors often came up beneath the porch where the children could see them. From then on I had another job. The children would give me an anna or two and ask me to go down and buy things for them. Usually it was something to eat, potato sticks or fruit. Sometimes the gubbara wala, the balloon seller, came and everyone wanted a small balloon.

I worked in the hospital all spring and summer until the end of July when I left to attend college, and during my vacation, the month of October. I looked forward to going to the hospital each afternoon. It was the high point in my day when I could forget myself and think and worry about other people, the little hospital people whose problems were so much greater than any I had ever known.

EIGHT

Along the Road

I went to and from the hospital each day by bicycle. It was a little over four miles each way and I could do it, if it were raining or if I were late, in less than a half hour. But usually it took me longer, often forty-five minutes, just because I, like almost everyone else, was in no hurry.

During the spring and summer months, when the thermometer often reached 115° in the shade, I left for the hospital soon after lunch. Some of my friends thought I was foolish to go out into the hot, midday sun. Conversely, I could never understand how anyone could be content to remain imprisoned within the four walls of a house. If I had not continued to work during those hot summer months, I know my mind, like theirs, would have been constantly on the heat and my own discomfort.

A leisurely bicycle ride in the open air seemed somehow refreshing to me and I found that a busy person rarely has a chance to notice his own discomfort. As long as I was busy, Delhi's heat did not bother me.

Leaving the house, I followed narrow, tree-lined Ratendon Road to its end. On my right was beautiful Lodhi Park and a colony of modern, two-storied apartment buildings. Big, single-storied upper-class homes lined the road on my left.

At the end of Ratendon Road a kindly-looking old man, with a snowy white beard, sold fruit in an open air shop—melon, watermelon, apples, a delicious grape-like fruit called leechies, mangoes, bananas or custard apples, depending upon the season. Nearby two small boys had bicycle repair equipment spread out on the side of the road underneath a big tree. They were always there when I went by, sleeping or playing or, occasionally, fixing bicycles.

At the end of Ratendon Road, I turned left onto a small lane which ended at one of the main roads, Prithviraj Road. Prithviraj Road was lined with low official-looking new stucco buildings, offices of the Indian government. At closing time there was as much bicycle traffic along that road as there is car traffic along Route 1 in Connecticut on a summery Sunday afternoon.

Prithviraj Road ran right up to a big circle with a statue of King Edward the Eighth still in the center. I bicycled around the circle until I got to Hardinge Road, which ran, a few blocks further on, into Mathra Road, the main road between Old and New Delhi. From there it was about two miles to the hospital.

In the heat of the early summer afternoon these roads were almost deserted. But in the evening when I came home there was always a bustle of traffic—a few people walking, hundreds more on bicycles, dozens of horse-drawn tonga carts, bullock carts from the outlying villages, occasionally a cart pulled by a haughty, slow-moving camel, plus some trucks, buses and cars. There were so many bicycles that we had to use hand signals just like the drivers of the automobiles.

I always had a feeling of great independence and excitement when I was on my bicycle. Coming home, on Mathra Road, there is a long sloping hill and everybody on bicycles usually went down at top speed. Like children we would zoom past each other and past the slower moving carts, oblivious of the cars that raced past us.

When I first went along Mathra Road in 1951, there was much open land on either side of the road. When I left in 1953, buildings were going up all along. At the Old Delhi end of Mathra Road there is a big stadium, on the right, where the cricket and hockey matches are played, and a jail and a Jain rest house on the left. Often when I passed the jail I saw groups of prisoners, their feet chained together, walking along the road carrying picks and shovels, supervised by two or three khaki dressed policemen.

Beyond the Jain rest house and the stadium is a big intersection where Mathra Road runs past the Delhi gate into Old Delhi. The hospital is on the left, sprawled along the intersecting road, Circular Road, for almost a quarter of a mile.

I left my bike with others in a bicycle park within the hospital grounds. The two men who watched the bicycles soon became my good friends. One, a shy, good-looking man who spoke only Hindustani, was interested in my work in the hospital. We talked about it and sometimes, also, about America.

The other, an older man, took it upon himself to improve my Hindustani. His own speech was a wonderful mixture of English and Hindustani. When he came to a word that he didn't know in English, he would say it in Hindustani. He used to call me Baby.

I paid these men two annas every day (about three cents), as did everyone who left his bicycle in a bicycle park. But often as not I would forget to bring any money. Then the older man would smile and say, "Don't worry about it, Baby. You can bring it tomorrow." More than once I borrowed money from them to fix a flat tire.

Having a flat tire was almost an everyday experience for me, especially during the summer when the hot tar and cement of the road weakened the rubber. I rode a rented bike until May and was always having trouble with it. The tires had continual leaks and the chain often came off. In the daytime there was usually a bicycle repairman nearby, for their little shops were set up every half mile or so along the road. But at night I had less luck.

A bicycle repairman could pack up and move his shop whenever business was getting slow in a particular spot. When he found a better place he would merely have to lay his equipment down at the side of the road, usually beneath a shady tree. That would be his shop for the day.

Most of these bicycle repairmen treated me as just another bicycler, not as an American who could afford to be overcharged. The going rate was two annas for each patch, air for half an anna or free. The bicycle man near our house would patch my tires whether or not I had money with me, knowing that I would be back in a day or two and would pay him then.

One day on the way to the hospital, as a result of a slight collision, my front wheel was badly bent. I took it to the nearest bicycle shop and explained to the man that I did not have enough money to pay but could bring him whatever I owed him the next day. Although he worked a good twenty minutes on it he told me not to bother about the money. When I came the next day to pay him he was gone.

Except for the expense I never really minded all those flat tires. But there was one thing about bicycle riding which I minded very much and which, at times, made me dread to go out of the house. On June 20th I was exasperated by it and wrote in my diary: "Friendly, friendly India. But I am tired of the staring."

I could never get accustomed to the staring. It became less as the months went by, as people grew used to seeing me. Eventually the bicycle repairmen, the old man who sold the fruit, the policemen, and other "regulars" scarcely bothered to look up when I passed. But to the hundreds of pedestrians and other bicyclers the sight of a girl, particularly a non-Indian girl in Indian clothes, was unusual and they looked me up and down.

Today there are far more young women on Delhi streets than there were ten years ago. But girl bicyclers are not yet a common sight and are rarely seen on the streets after dark. I am sure that many people considered me quite immodest. I remember one contemptuous-looking woman who spat in front of my bicycle as I went by her.

Perhaps this is one reason why the nursing profession is still not fully respected in India. Nurses, especially public health nurses, visit homes, often alone, on their bicycles and on the road are open to abuse from passers-by. Many old-fashioned people have assumed, on seeing this, that nurses generally are immodest. It is no wonder, therefore, that more women go into medicine, a profession that is respected, than into nursing.

The good things of bicycle riding, however, far outweighed the staring which I disliked so much. Most of all I liked the independence, the feeling that I did not have to rely on someone else to take me wherever I wanted to go. The bicycle was mine, the time of day was mine. I could come and go more or less as I pleased.

Also when I was on my bicycle I felt a part of the slow-moving life of the Indian street, not isolated from it as I felt in a car. I saw all sorts of people, of things, of happenings. When the first welcome rain of the monsoon came that summer I was on my bicycle on my way home from the hospital. By the time I reached home I was soaked to the skin, but happily soaked. It was the first rain in months and I and everything else had been hot and dry. Maybe it looked funny, but not many bicyclers hurried for shelter that day.

One day, as I was riding home from the hospital along Mathra Road I heard a voice from behind me call "Bahenji." I stopped and a nice-looking young woman dressed in the full-gathered skirts of a villager, came up to me and asked where I was going. She said she was tired and wondered if I could take her part of the way. I did, leaving her where the road to her village turned off to the left. She still had a mile or two to walk.

Soon after I started work at the hospital, at the beginning of April, the Hindu festival of Ramnaumi was celebrated in Delhi. Near Delhi Gate and the stadium, on Mathra Road, a big fair had been organized. On my way to the hospital that day I passed bullock cart after bullock cart slowly coming into the fair from the nearby villages. Each cart was filled with laughing, singing village people, the women dressed gaily in bright orange, red and yellow saries pulled modestly over their heads, the men dressed in more somber white.

Along the road small, hastily constructed but brilliantly decorated stalls had been set up. Sweets, fruit, ice-cream and fried foods were arranged temptingly to lure passersby. Many of the stalls were piled high with toys and small painted clay images of the gods and goddesses. Vendors peddled their wares among the crowd already gathered on the fair grounds, calling out in loud voices what they had to sell.

A loud-speaker blared out the latest popular tunes. The music of a small merry-go-round competed weakly. Barefoot children chased each other in and out among the stands, stood solemnly sucking popsicles or sat sedately in the ferris wheel with older brothers and sisters.

I told my hospital children about the fair when I finally reached them. They could hear the loudspeaker from the ward and spoke longingly of the fun they could be having.

Every so often, going to or from the hospital, I got caught in a dust storm. The dust storms, which were quite common during the hot, dry months of May and June, usually came quickly and went quickly. But while they lasted they were no fun. Generally a heavy wind came with them and I found it hard to stay on my bike. Most of the time I resignedly got off, but sometimes I stubbornly kept on, perhaps for the excitement of it, covering my face with my chunni, my long scarf.

My chunni was the cause of a couple of embarrassing moments. Usually I wore it so that it hung down either side of my back. I had not thought that it was long enough to get caught in the bicycle wheel. But one day it did, somehow winding round and round the chain apparatus. I knew it was unheard of for a girl to be seen in public without her chunni and with much embarrassment I lifted the bike up to the side of the road and tried to unravel and unwind the now greasy and much torn chunni. I was thankful for the young man who came up and unwound it for me.

It always amazed me how much a bicycle could carry. For many families, the father's bicycle was the only means of transportation. On Sundays and holidays you could see scores of bicycles "filled to capacity," the father sitting on the seat, a small child in a basket on the handlebars, the mother on the back fender with another child in her lap. Once I saw a mother and father and three children all on the same cycle, the third child sitting on the crossbar.

The milk men coming in from the villages carried two and more huge cans of milk. The fruit and vegetable sellers balanced huge baskets of fruit or vegetables on either side of their bicycles. You could hardly see the men who sold the little straw chairs. The chairs were piled one upon another on their bicycles in some miraculous fashion so that they nearly hid the vendors. If a man was careful, he could even carry a charpoi bed, tied precariously on the fender.

Although I went to and from the hospital daily, the ride never became boring. There were always new things to see, new people to meet, new things to learn. And the staring that made me so uncomfortable was the only price I had to pay for the ride.

NINE

A Delhi Week End

WHILE I WAS in school there was a feeling about a week end in Delhi much like that of a week end at home in America. Monday, Tuesday, Wednesday, Thursday and Friday were busy work days. Children went to school, men went to their work, the shops were open and bustling with activity, the bazaars were noisy and crowded, and the parks, except in the evening, were empty.

Saturday came and the pace slowed down. Children stayed home from school, most men went to work only in the morning, many of the shops were closed in the afternoon, and the parks were crowded as soon as it became cool.

With Sunday, the activity of the week came to a stop. The family was together. There could be picnics, visiting, or parties; or the afternoon could be spent in the shade of a big neem tree in one of the many parks, or on a charpoi—asleep. The bazaars were often busy; Friday is the day of rest and worship for the Mohammedans. But most of the city had a Sunday feeling about it.

Although I worked at the hospital daily, Saturdays and Sundays as well as week days, the week ends were different for me too. Saturday mornings I worked in a small clinic near our house.

This clinic, operated by a group of Indian women with help from Delhi's American women's club, was one of many in New Delhi and Delhi. Other clinics in the city, most of them maternity and child welfare centers, are operated by the goverment. The clinic in which I worked was attended mainly by women and children, most of whom lived in the neighborhood.

The doctor, the two women who filled his prescriptions and gave out medicine, and the two who worked in the treatment room, were volunteers. The medicine was bought by the club, and the powdered milk which we gave to the children was a gift of UNICEF.

The first time a patient came to the clinic he was charged two annas, or about three cents, no matter what his ailment. Besides helping to pay some of the expenses of the clinic, I think this charge gave the patient a feeling that the medicine and treatment were not simply being handed out to him. It helped him to realize that he would be expected to accept his well-being as his own responsibility.

The doctor sat at a table on the porch of the small building. The patient first came to him and described his ailment. The doctor diagnosed it and wrote out the treatment and/or medicine which the patient should have, advising him to return the next day the clinic was open (three times a week) or not, as the case might be.

If the patient needed medicine, he went from the doctor to the window where medicine was being given out; here he gave the volunteer his prescription and a bottle for the medicine, receiving in turn his medicine and complete instructions as to how to use it. If he had a cut, a boil, an infection of some kind, a sore throat, sore eyes or a burn, he would go from the prescription window to the treatment room where he would be treated.

I enjoyed working in the treatment room where I could come to know the patients and actually see and help to cure their ailments. After a while I became expert at putting drops in eyes, painting throats and bandaging.

Painting throats, however, was not my favorite job. One of the first times I did it I had not wound the cotton tightly enough around the stick and the cotton and the throat medicine found their way down into the poor child's stomach. I was horribly embarrassed and sorry for the little girl who gagged and hastily accepted a glass of water. Happily, everyone was sympathetic and the girl recovered quickly. But I felt sure that she would be back in a few days with something dreadfully wrong with her stomach. Fortunately she did not return.

Usually I worked in the prescription department where I soon became acquainted with the boxes and bottles of pills which lined the shelves, and the big quart bottles of liquid medicine which covered most of the table on which we worked. One of the medicines we gave out most often was a red, pepperminty liquid which the doctor secretly called "psychology" medicine.

We usually treated at least fifty persons a morning at the small clinic, often more. It was different from the hospital in that I could actually help the patient medically. It was a wonderful way, I thought, to spend a Saturday morning.

Saturday afternoons I worked as usual at the hospital. But there was time in between that and the clinic to have lunch with friends, or afterwards, to go on a picnic, to a movie or to a friend's house for the evening. Often, however, I spent the time at home, reading, writing or doing homework.

My room was a very small room on the street side of the house. I usually sat at a table in front of the open window where the sound of Ratendon Road and the streets beyond came in to me and served as a pleasant background for my work. The cheerful bells of the tonga carts, the rhythmic squeaking of a bullock cart, the twang, twang of a portable cotton carding machine as its owner walked past, the happy chattering of small children, the shouting of one man to another, the song or whistle of a passing cyclist, the mournful tune of the snake charmer's horn, the gay strains of a harmonica, birds singing, a dog barking and, at night, the eerie cries of the jackals (wild dogs) in the park behind our house were by and large Indian sounds, and I knew and loved each one of them.

Sunday was often a busy day. Early in the morning we sometimes went bird watching. For lunch or supper we might go on a picnic. And in the afternoon there was usually something going on; once it was a sports meet, another time a Girl Scout rally, another, an election meeting and a movie. In the first months of our Delhi stay there was sight-seeing.

As I had always been interested in being able to recognize different kinds of birds at home, I very much enjoyed the Delhi bird-watching expeditions. We went with a group of Delhi people—English, American and Indian—usually to a deserted place outside of the city, near a pond or river or in the "jungle."

The first Sunday we went to a beautiful place on the banks of the Jumna River near a ripe field of tall-standing sugar cane. It was early in the morning. The sky was bright, the foliage plentiful and green. There were many birds, both water and land. We saw the more common birds—the mynah, the big, black ugly crow and the sly, high-flying pariah kite, and others—the lovely, long-tailed, brown and white tree-pie, the perky little chickadee-like grey tit, the talkative babbler, many of the bulbul family, the trim black and white dhayal, the beautiful black-headed yellow oriole, the multi-colored roller, the brilliant blue and orange king-fisher, the fan-headed hoopoe and the noisy parakeets.

Another day we went to a place on the other side of the city, passing over the Jumna River via the Jumna Bridge. There was a bad traffic jam at the bridge. Steb and I spent a wonderful half hour while waiting our turn to go over, watching the innumerable vehicles of the Indian road unravel themselves from the confusion. There were people walking, hundreds of bikes, horse-pulled tonga carts, bullock carts, little carts pulled by men, often filled with coal, automobiles, trucks—empty ones headed out of Delhi for the Punjab, others filled with produce headed into Delhi—buses, herds of sheep, water buffalo, goats and cattle and even a camel train, seldom seen in that part of the country.

Down under the bridge, on the banks of the river, washermen were washing the clothes of the people of the city. The grass along the edge of the river was covered with the freshly-washed clothing, drying in the hot sun.

The washerman's work is hot and tiring. Each had a narrow slab of stone half in the water, on which he beat the clothing. Raising the article he was washing far over his head, he would slam it down again and again against the rock.

The bird watching that Sunday was apparently not as interesting to me as the Jumna River Bridge jam-up because I remember none of it.

Often for Sunday lunch or supper my family or my friends went on a picnic. Lodhi Park, right out in back of our house, was the nearest of the picnic places and we went there frequently. I loved its coolness, its shady greenery and its quietness. Its gates were open day and night and there were almost always people there: families picnicking, father playing with young sons and daughters, women sitting on the grass talking, students reading and resting, a working man taking an afternoon siesta, children playing.

I remember one Sunday that we bicycled to Hauz Kauz, another picnic place much like Lodhi Park, four or five miles outside the city. It was beautiful there, grassy and shady and filled with other Sunday picnickers. Big families—grandmothers, grandfathers, mothers, fathers, aunts, uncles and many children—sat on blankets laid out in the shade of the trees. Young boys had organized volleyball games. Groups of students sat talking, playing the radio. Someone had brought his harmonium and another his sitar. There was a wonderfully happy, carefree atmosphere.

Hauz Kauz was even more beautiful at night. Sometimes on a Sunday night we took a picnic there. The place was quiet and deserted, brightened only by the moon.

Something almost always came up to keep me busy on Sunday afternoons, before or after I went to the hospital. One afternoon we watched a hockey match between an Indian team and one from Japan. The Indian team was very good, playing with speed and great skill. We cheered it on to victory.

Another day I attended a Girl Guide rally in honor of Miss Crowe, an American who was touring parts of the world on behalf of the Scout World Fellowship. I wore my blue mariner uniform. The Indian girls were dressed in the scout uniform of India—white salvar and cumeez and a blue dapatta.

In January of 1952 India held her first national elections. In Delhi parades and public meetings were common and billboards and posters advertised the different parties and candidates. One Sunday in the middle of the month Steb and I went to a Congress Party election meeting in Old Delhi. When we arrived, Nehru, who was to speak, had not yet come. The park was crowded with thousands of people—men, women and children, and vendors selling all sorts of good-looking things to eat. We joined them, edging as near to the speaker's platform as we could.

At very nearly the expected time Nehru's car drove up. A murmur went through the crowd. There was no clapping or wild cheering, simply a quiet acknowledgement of the great man's arrival. Nehru spoke in Hindustani—slowly and clearly. Unfortunately we had not yet learned enough of the language to understand all that he said.

Since I could not understand Nehru's speech it was the members of the crowd and the behavior of the crowd as a whole which interested me most. The individuals that made up the crowd were of different social and economic classes, different religions, and moreover different castes, who were united by their common interest in Nehru, or Punditji, as he is commonly called. To the city public, I realized, caste had little importance.

With so much to do—clinic work, hospital work, picnics, sports matches, and seeing friends—it was hard for me to be idle on a week end in Delhi. While school was in session it was a much looked-forward-to two days, just as it is to me now, at Oberlin College.

TEN

A Week in a Village

MY INTEREST in nursing led me to wonder what kind of nursing and public health work was being done in the villages. My curiosity in turn led me to inquire at the College of Nursing in New Delhi whether it would be possible for me to stay for a week or so at the village of Chawla, twenty miles west of Delhi in Delhi state. I had heard that nursing students from the college were living and working in this village. I was happy when they said "yes."

When I arrived at Chawla near lunchtime on a hot June day, the nurses had not yet come back from their daily visits to the village homes. Miss Craig, a friend of mine from the college, showed me around the nurses' compound. Four tiny, one- or two-room prefabricated houses were set at the edge of the village, one for cooking, eating and recreation, one for the staff and two for the students.

There were eight nurses at the village at that time—six students, a graduate doing research on village nutrition and a young supervisor. The students were doing this village health work as part of their nursing training.

Most of them had come from North India—the Punjab, Delhi, Uttar Pradesh or Bihar—two were from Bengal and one from Ceylon. Living with these girls, representatives of different parts of India, was a new and valuable experience as was living and working in the village itself.

When the girls came back from the village we had lhassi, a drink made of curds and water. It was very good, cooling and cheap. I learned that the villagers drink much of it. A short while later we had lunch, an Indian meal of rice and chappaties and vegetable curry. The girls ate skillfully with their fingers as I had learned to do at Suman's and at Sevagram.

After lunch until about 4:00, during the greatest heat of the day, the girls rested or slept as do most people during the hot months in India. Late in the afternoon we had tea and milk and from then until it became dark the girls worked in the village or stayed at the compound making health posters or writing reports.

In the late afternoon of my first day at Chawla I went into the village with two of the students. The village people were used to seeing the nurses and said friendly "namaste's" as we passed; many invited us to sit and talk for a while.

The first child we visited had a fever and was a strange case. She was only about four days old and, as is so often the case, unwanted because she was a girl. According to custom her father would have to pay a dowry (gifts demanded by a husband's family of the bride's family) at the time of her marriage. He had little enough money at it was.

The baby was not getting proper food or care. The nurses bathed her and gave her some water but there was not much else they could do. They urged the mother to care for her properly and feed her more often. The baby was sickly and weak and would probably die if the mother did not follow the nurses' advice.

The next case was a young boy with typhoid, a common disease in India usually caused by contamination of food, water or milk. There was one other case of it in the village.

The boy was in a tiny dark room of the small house, sleeping on a charpoi, his little sister sitting beside him, fanning him. Under the supervision of the nurses he was receiving good care, medicine and treatment. Otherwise he might have died as many of the villagers had before the nurses came.

I wondered how they could keep such infectious patients isolated. I learned that many Hindus still believe that such contagious diseases, especially smallpox, are the result of the wrath of a goddess. In many cases the sick person is considered possessed with evil spirits, and people are usually unwilling to come near him.

After these visits we walked around the village, stopping to talk with some of the women here and there. Many were spinning, others watching babies or preparing food. They were extremely friendly and the extent to which they accepted the nurses was amazing.

The nurses were outsiders—foreigners to the village. Instead of the familiar full gathered skirts of the village women, they wore shining clean, white saries. They acted "immodestly" before the village men, not covering their faces or even their heads in the men's presence. Why, most of them were still unmarried and yet they did not try to avoid the men's eyes. Most of them could speak but a little of the village language and among themselves they spoke a language the village people couldn't understand.

Moreover, these nurses suggested that the village people do things unheard of in village history and that they stop doing other things they and their ancestors before them had done for centuries. Why, everyone had always known that to feed a baby water before it was a month old would cause it to have a bloated stomach. And imagine putting a piece of white cloth smeared with smelly yellow stuff on a cut instead of a cool layer of mud. Then too, some said that a baby would have convulsions and die if he were put down in the strange metal thing the nurses say is a scale.

These and similar attitudes faced the nurses when they first arrived at the village. By no means have these superstitions been completely overcome but little by little they are growing less common.

As we walked down the village lanes, the nurses laughed and talked with the women sitting in the doorways of their homes. They admired their clothes and babies. If a woman had troubles that she wished to discuss with the nurses, the nurses listened patiently and answered sympathetically.

In this way they had first gained the villagers' confidence. Then perhaps one of the braver women had given water to her baby and saw that his stomach did not become bloated; or had cautiously allowed her baby to be put on the scales and saw that he did not have convulsions. And when the nurses came to weigh him again a month later the mother could actually see that her baby had grown.

The nurses' job was difficult, often discouraging. But the daily victories, tiny as they were, gave them courage to go on.

Chawla is a village of about 1,500 people, concentrated in a small area. The village is bigger than most in India, the average being about 700 people. The houses, generally made of blocks of mud mixed with straw and coated with a smooth layer of mud, are built one against another. Occasionally the homes of the more wealthy are substantially built of wood and brick.

The average home is small, consisting of two or three tiny dark rooms and an open courtyard, the center of household activity. The many family members eat, work and sleep in the courtyard and often share it with a cow or water buffalo. In a corner is the fireplace stove. Usually there is a charpoi or two where the women can rest from their work and sit and talk, and the men can sit in the evenings, smoking a common hookah pipe and discussing village, national and sometimes international events.

In the two or three tiny rooms off the courtyard, the farm supplies, grain for the animals, and family belongings are kept. There are rarely windows and the rooms are dark. The homes are generally very clean. The hard packed mud floors are swept daily and the brass cooking and eating utensils are usually spotless.

Rarely, however, does the villager's sense of cleanliness go beyond his front door. A man takes trouble not to spit on the floor of his courtyard but carefully goes to the door and spits into the street. He makes sure that dirty waste water flows out of his house—into the street. To instill in the villagers a feeling of community responsibility—a social consciousness—was one of the nurses' big problems.

As in most villages in India, there are different castes in Chawla, each occupying its own section of the village. The people of the various castes are fairly friendly and free with each other but eating together and intermarriage are still taboo.

My first morning at Chawla, I was awakened by the bells of the bullocks as they were driven to work in the fields. It was only 6:00 but I felt like a sleepyhead. I knew that the farmers had been plowing, the housewives drawing water from the well and doing other chores, and their children playing, since daylight. The villagers rise with the sun and work early in the day while it is cool. It was the plowing season, just before the monsoon rains, and a busy time for the men and boys.

We had slept outside where it was cool and my friends were already up, folding their bedding and bathing. There was no electricity or running water in the village. Water was carried in pails and big brass and earthen containers to our compound and to the village homes from wells on the outskirts of the village, sometimes over a half mile away.

It is usually the women who bring the water from the wells. Balancing an earthen jar, full to the brim with water, on her covered head, her full skirt swishing, her jewelry jingling and her dark eyes dancing, the Indian village woman seems to have stepped out of a book. She is strong and gay and colorful. Her skirt, reaching just above her ankles, is tightly ·gathered, full and graceful. The material is usually a bright-colored print. Besides the skirt she wears a loose shirt and a large, also brightly-colored, shawl which covers her head and sometimes her entire face.

At the time of her marriage, a girl is given much jewelry—bangles, armlets and anklets, nose pierces, earrings, hair ornaments and necklaces—most of which is heavy, beautifully ornamented silver. This jewelry is purchased at great expense by her family and is a cause of much of the load of debt under which the villager lives and dies.

By 7:00 we had had our breakfast of purathas—a kind of fried chappatie—cut up and seasoned boiled potatoes, and milk or tea, and the girls were ready for their day's work. They ran a daily clinic in a building of the compound with the help of a woman doctor coming from the nearby town of Najafgarh once a week. That morning I went with them to the clinic and helped in the treatment department.

The health service which they provide, paid for by the College of Nursing, reaches every Chawla villager. Most of the Chawla children up to five years of age have complete card records started if possible at their birth, on which their medical history is kept. These include notes from home and clinic visits and show weight increases from month to month.

When a woman becomes pregnant a new card is begun on which the results of monthly examinations are written. Also on these cards are written the names and state of health or cause of death, of previous children. For instance:

Name: Shanti Devi
Previous children:

Name	Sex	Date of birth	Health	Death cause	Age at death
Usha	fem.	1944	good		
Ram Lal	m.	1945		typhoid	4 years
Hari Ram	m.	1947		pneumonia	6 months
Pushpa	fem.	1949	fever		
Mohinder	m.	1951	good		

June 5, 1952—20 weeks pregnant

The health service has certainly decreased the death rate of babies at birth and children in infancy. But still, babies and children die. In all India 50% die before they are 12 and one-fourth die in their first year of life. One trouble is that the villagers do not get enough food of the right kind. Some of them treat their young children carelessly and few understand the importance of cleanliness.

I do not think that they generally suffer from lack of food, particularly now with the increase in India's food production within the last few years. But their diet is often deficient in vegetables, fruits and high-protein foods. Heavy foods—grain and fats—make up the biggest part of what they eat. The Chawla villagers are Hindus, almost all strict vegetarians who will eat neither meat nor eggs.

Except for a grain store, there is no place in Chawla where the villagers can buy food. A man selling vegetables occasionally comes through the village but he cannot be relied upon to come regularly. The town of Najafgarh is three miles up the road and the people of Chawla and the surrounding villages often make the trips to the bazaar there—by cycle, on foot or in their bullock carts—to buy vegetables and fruit.

One day three of the nurses and myself cycled into Najafgarh to shop, like the villagers, in the bazaar, and to help in another clinic there. Besides this clinic there is a new hospital at Najafgarh which now serves 28 villages in the surrounding area and will later be expanded to serve the whole district.

After working for a few hours in the clinic we bought vegetables and fruit in the crowded bazaar. The prices were amazingly low by American standards. For instance, we bought three melons for five annas or six cents. There were many kinds of vegetables in the bazaar shops—tomatoes, potatoes, cucumbers, pumpkins, okra, beans and onions—and fruits—bananas, coconuts, melons, plums, mangoes, peaches and leechies. Vendors were selling molds of crushed ice over which sweet fruit syrup had been poured—a treat especially popular with the children.

Most of the days that I spent at Chawla I went with one of the nurses on her regular visits to the village homes. We visited the small girl who was not wanted almost daily. Within a week she was a little better. The nurse, Hackie, usually washed the baby and gave it some water and medicine. We learned that the husband refused to see the mother for another month and a half. It was her fault that a baby girl had been born!

One day we stopped at the home of a family who had allowed the nutrition research student to weigh their small baby weekly since his birth. This was one of the more progressive families of the community. The women of the house were exceptionally healthy and friendly and accepted the advice of the nurses without question.

One morning after a cool and sound sleep, I was awakened by someone calling. It must have been about 4:30; the light was just coming. "Missahib, Missahibji" (a term of respect given to young women). We were all sleeping close together outside and apparently the others had heard it too.

"Kya hogya?" (What's happened?), I heard one of the nurses say, and then, "Hackie, get up quick. It's Lakshmi's case."

Lakshmi was a pregnant woman Hackie and I had visited the day before. Her baby was due the first week of June. A relative of hers had come to tell us that Lakshmi's baby was coming. Hackie and the supervisor left at once.

They returned a while later. A healthy baby boy had been born at 9:45, weight, seven and a half pounds.

Later in the morning we visited the house of the new

baby. I had wondered how a delivery could take place with any privacy in the small crowded house. A charpoi had been screened off in one corner of one of the small rooms. But despite this I learned from my friend that there was little privacy and that village children knew much about such matters.

There Lakshmi lay, her seven-hour-old son beside her. I held him while Hackie fed him a little water. The next day when we visited him again Hackie taught me how to wash him and I did it. Neighborhood women and children were rejoicing outside the door. If the baby had been a girl there would probably have been little such rejoicing.

One night after supper one of the nurses and I went into the village to the home of a girl who had just been married. At about 7:00 in the morning her bridegroom had come. We had seen him when he passed by the compound. He had come from a nearby village (most of the marriages are inter-village) at the head of a short procession of bullock carts which carried his friends and relatives.

Leading the procession was a band which had probably played the whole way. This procession in which the bridegroom comes to the bride on the day of the wedding is called the barat. I had witnessed it before in Delhi with Suman. This village bridegroom, however, did not have a yellow convertible.

The procession had arrived at the edge of the village and waited until one of the bride's family had come and greeted the bridegroom and his family with folded hands and the common greeting of the villagers—"Jai Ram"— Hail to God—before it continued on to the bride's house. There ceremonies and feasting lasted the whole day.

When we visited the bride in the evening the bridegroom and his party had eaten their dinner and gone. We were invited into the house and found the bride sitting with her mother and two other women in a corner of the courtyard. She was having her hair braided into many tiny braids. She looked about sixteen and was very pretty. Because she was a daughter of the village and because her husband and his guests had left, her face was uncovered. She explained this to us, saying that the men sitting outside the door talking were her "brothers" so she needn't cover her face.

Tomorrow her husband would come again and take her away to his village and home in the evening. There she would stay for three days among his people, days of feasting and more ceremonies, and then she would return to her village alone for six to eight months. She would then go to her husband's place to live permanently. There she would not be a daughter of the village and her face would remain covered in the presence of men.

The time a girl remains in her village after marriage depends upon her age. For instance, we met another girl who was married when she was nine and at eighteen was still living in Chawla away from her husband. Soon, I expect, she will go to her husband's home.

Most of the marriages take place when the girl is from nine to fifteen years old. This is what we in America hear and as a result we are inclined to criticize the Indian people for their "child marriages." But as the young public health supervisor told me, "It all comes to the same thing. In this area, at least, the bride usually will not live with her husband, before she is seventeen or eighteen and rarely does a girl have children before she is one or two years older."

Recently a law was passed prohibiting girls from marrying before they are fifteen. Boys must be eighteen.

To me, Chawla was beautiful. Life there was, of necessity, extremely simple. The complicated and often unnecessary wheels of modern societies did not turn there, and as a result I felt somehow that man was closer both to his fellow man and to nature. There was more dependence on other people and upon the earth, the rain and the animals. For me this atmosphere was a happy one.

The village homes, roughly finished and the same color as the earth, the mutkas of baked clay, the wooden plow, the homespun cotton clothing, were simple and an obvious part of the nature from which they had come. For this reason they were beautiful to me.

And there was a wonderful quietness, not a stillness

exactly, but a quietness punctuated by such lovely sounds as a cattle bell tinkling, a dog barking, a bird singing, a quiet voice, the music of a reed flute. An occasional truck passing by the village on its way to Najafgarh on the usually quiet road was the only motor sound.

I, as an outsider, found beauty, friendliness, and quiet at Chawla. But had I been born in that village, had I grown up illiterate and sometimes hungry when the crops were not as big as had been hoped for, and, as a young person, had gone away from the village and seen the comforts of the other people, perhaps then I would have been able to feel only hatred for the village way of life.

Then I might not have been able to find the same beauty and quiet where people suffered—I had found—unnecessarily. And either I would have gone away from the village and lived in the city, more appealing because it gave comforts I would never have dreamed of in the village, or I would have returned to help my people.

Unnecessary disease and ill health are ugly. Hunger is ugly. Illiteracy and ignorance are ugly. Perhaps it was because I, an outsider, had never had to experience their ugliness and because I knew that people were trying hard to erase the ugliness, that I could see beauty in the village.

ELEVEN

College Life

DELHI PUBLIC SCHOOL closed the middle of May for summer vacation. I left it gladly and determined not to return in August when it would reopen. What I would do during the coming school year I was not certain. I had not lived for any period of time outside of Delhi, which I now considered my home, and therefore felt unfamiliar with the rest of the country. There was the question, too, of how long I should interrupt my classroom education.

I had heard of a university in West Bengal, about a hundred miles north of Calcutta, where the study of Indian culture was emphasized. I was happy when I was accepted there as a special student.

The university, whose name, Santiniketan, means the "abode of peace," was founded by the great poet, author, artist and musician, Rabrindranath Tagore. Tagore remained the guiding spirit of Santiniketan until his death in 1941. In the part of his autobiography entitled *My School*, Tagore wrote:

. . . The young mind should be saturated with the idea that it has been born in a human world which is in harmony with the world around it. And this is what our regular type of school ignores with an air of superior wisdom, severe and disdainful. . . .

We have come to this world to accept it, not merely to know it. We may become powerful by knowledge, but we attain fullness by sympathy. The highest education is that which does not merely give us information but makes our life in harmony with existence. But we find that the education of sympathy is not only systematically ignored in schools, but it is severely repressed. . . . We rob the child of his earth to teach him geography, of language to teach him grammar. . . . Child nature protests against such calamity with all its power of suffering, subdued at last into silence by punishment.

However, since Tagore's death in 1941 and the authorization of Santiniketan as a government-supported university, the college of the university has been brought, unfortunately I think, somewhat more into line with the regular British-type colleges in India. Yet there is still much of the spirit of Tagore there and it was for this reason and to take advantage of the art and music schools that I decided on going to Santiniketan.

The school year at Santiniketan began the middle of July. But because no one seemed to care or insist on punctuality, and because I felt in no hurry to leave Delhi, I arrived a few days late.

It seemed strange to leave Delhi. There was much

about the city that I disliked, such as its westernized and somewhat artificial atmosphere. I disliked the staring and the conspicuousness that seemed to be my lot when I moved amongst people I did not know.

But Delhi was home to me and it was hard to leave the things I loved about it—the crowded bazaars, my hospital children, the people like Suman and Shakur and the other servants who had become my good friends—and, of course, my family. It was not easy to leave them all behind and set out on the twenty-six hour train journey to Bolpur, the nearest station to Santiniketan.

Steb came with me on the train. We had reserved two of the six seats in a second-class compartment and as we sped along in the direction of Calcutta I studied the other people who were travelling with us. (In a railway compartment everyone studies everyone else I think.) There were two young Indian girls, very friendly and cheerful, who were going to Lucknow to study at a girls' college. They wore plain white cotton saries and each had plaited her beautiful black hair into two long braids.

A third seat was occupied by a stiff-haired, middle-aged English woman travelling to Kanpur. "I'll be getting off at about tea time," she told us.

And there were two other passengers, a plump and greying Punjabi grandmother and her slim, lovely granddaughter. They were probably refugees from the Punjab who had made their home in Delhi. They spoke little and, like the rest of us, slept much of the time.

At "tea time," just as the English woman had forewarned, we slid into the station at Kanpur. She and the two students left us here. It was after dark when we got to Allahabad, near Benaras, and the two Punjabis got off, leaving Steb and me an empty compartment for the night.

In the morning we were in a new land, rice-growing Bengali, green and wet. In some fields men were plowing, the water up to their ankles, and in others green rice shoots were being transplanted. In contrast the land we had come from was generally brown and dry.

In the stations we noticed that the language and script were different than those in Delhi. Billboards advertised

Colgate tooth-paste, English-made biscuits, Indian cement, and other products in Bengali, a sister tongue to Hindi. People spoke in soft, musical tones.

The clothing of the people was different, too, from what we had become accustomed to seeing in Delhi. Men wore the dhoti, a sheet-like garment wrapped intricately around the body. The women wore saries instead of the salvar and cumeez as I did.

We changed trains at Burdwan in Bengal, in mid-morning. Again the compartment was full but I was too sleepy to study my fellow-travellers carefully. Two were Indian businessmen, I surmised, and there was a young, recently married couple, the bride shy in her brilliant red sari and elaborate jewelry.

We arrived at Bolpur and the university just before lunch. Steb left soon after and I was taken to my room in the section of the girl's dormitory in which the art students lived. There were about thirty students living there, most of them in double rooms, a few in singles.

Although my room was for two girls, I did not get a roommate until August. The second-story room was small, with plain white-washed walls and an uncarpeted stone floor. It was furnished with two low, table-like beds on which a thin mattress was put, two tables and a stool. There were four windows, two open to the outside and two the hall, making the room light and airy. There was one weak electric light, unfit for studying at night. The room was simple and pleasant.

After I had unpacked, put my books, pictures and odds and ends on the shelves, my bedding and a colorful bedspread on the bed and arranged my clothing in the small trunk, the room looked more my own and I knew I was going to like living in it.

A couple of days after my arrival, as I was sitting at the table in my room studying, I heard the "thump, thump" of something running across the roof. It stopped over my window and I saw a black hand reach down, followed quickly by the fuzzy brown body of a big monkey. He perched on my window sill and examined me and my room for some time. Then, as quickly as he had come, he left. It seemed to me that he was the room inspector, for I knew he called on the other girls too. I hoped that I had passed his test and would not be the subject of his gossiping.

Other wildlife also visited me in my room—birds, lizards, dogs and insects of every possible description. A mynah bird had a nest in a niche in the wall and often came in and sat on it. I know the crows came in when I was not around, looking for food. The lizards came out at night, small ones and large ones; they ran up and down the walls, catching insects. We carefully avoided each other.

The dogs wandered at random through the dormitory, homeless dogs with stomachs enlarged by the food they stole from the kitchen. Outside in the grass beneath my window two cows were tied and chickens wandered freely about.

I quickly adapted myself to the life of Santiniketan. It was a busy life. I awoke a little before 5:00 each day to the tune of chattering and singing hostel-mates. It was cool then and just beginning to get light.

At about 6:00 we had breakfast in the big eating hall where we sat on narrow benches at low wooden tables. The meals consisted of cocoa and either fresh buttered bread sprinkled with sugar or puris (puffed up chappaties) and a vegetable curry.

After breakfast each day there was a short song-prayer meeting, led each week by a different group of students. The prayer was a silent one and the songs, written by Tagore, often resembled our own American folk songs.

I usually had two or three classes in the morning. At about 11:30 we had our lunch. At lunchtime the dining hall was divided into four sections. The boys and girls were separated, and the vegetarians and non-vegetarians. Most of the students were non-vegetarians, a majority of these Bengalis. Bengalis are seldom vegetarians and include much fish in their diet.

I always ate vegetarian food. In Essex we had had a small farm—a cow, pigs and chickens. I had helped take care of, and naturally grown fond of, the animals. It had saddened me that meat was such an important part of our diet and, although I doubt that I could have stopped eating it in a place when I was surrounded by none but meat-eating people, in India where vegetarianism is so common, it was easy for me to change my habits.

We were given a choice of chappaties, which the Punjabis, other North Indians and I usually took, or rice, which is the staple food of the Bengalis and South Indians. In addition there was a potato curry, and usually a vegetable curry, dhal and delicious sweetened curds of which I could never get enough. Some seasons of the year, when a particular vegetable was plentiful and cheap in the market, we would get it day after day and then, after a few weeks, would see almost none of it. We had cauliflower, spinach, eggplant, tomatoes, onions, okra, pumpkin and, always, potatoes. Although many of the girls said that the food was terrible compared with what they had at home, I liked it very much.

After lunch, for two or three hours, we had a rest and study period. Like many of the girls I usually slept during this time, somehow managing to wake before my first afternoon class. My classes continued until late in the afternoon.

After classes for a couple of hours there was a games period. Some of the girls took part in organized games, others went to the store, took walks or sat on the steps of the dormitory and talked.

I loved to go on walks with my new friends at this beautiful time of day when the cloudless blue sky was streaked with orange in the west. But the games were fun too. We played net ball, a game something like basketball which I had learned at Delhi Public School, ringtoss and throw ball, a game much like volleyball.

At 7:00 we were expected to be back in the dormitory for a roll call. We spent the early evening studying, practicing instruments or dancing, or attending one of the various lectures, meetings, or performances. Supper came about 8:30. We slept early, as soon as the singing, talking and shouting, typical, I guess, of any girls' dormitory, had quieted down.

Wednesday was Santiniketan's weekly holiday when students were free to do almost anything they liked. Somehow I remember Wednesdays at Santiniketan as bright, hot, sunshiny days when I could completely relax and enjoy the bright, hot sunshine. I remember having a mania for washing clothing and linen. I loved their washed, clean, fresh smell and the heat of the sun on my back as I hung them up to dry in the large, grassy courtyard.

It was a day, too, when I could catch up on all the things I had neglected to do during the week. Besides studying for my regular courses I could read non-course books. Sometimes I could persuade my friend, Vijoya, to give me a lesson in Bengali or she could persuade me to go on one of Santiniketan's many picnics with her. And, if I felt completely lazy, I could catch up on my sleep, that activity most thoroughly neglected during the week.

Each Wednesday morning there was a short inter-religious temple service which all of the students were expected to attend. The temple was a small square building with partially open sides and colored glass windows. Often by the time I arrived, the building was already filled with students and many of the boys and girls were sitting outside on the steps. The service consisted of singing, a prayer and a sermon by a priest in Bengali.

I never knew enough Bengali to be able to fully understand the service. So I used to make a point of getting a seat outside on the steps where I could see the post office, the trees and fields of Santiniketan, the occasional activity on the road that went by the school to a nearby village, and think my own thoughts.

Often, as I looked out across Santiniketan's campus, I thought that it was not really beautiful. Perhaps it was the university buildings which kept it from being so. Almost all of them were old, concrete-brick, one- or two-storied structures of little or no architectural beauty. These buildings housed the living quarters, offices, library, museum, stores, theater, and the various schools of the university—the school of art, school of music, the college (we had, however, our college classes outdoors), school of Chinese studies, the school of Hindi studies, and the post graduate department.

But there was a lively quietness and restfulness about the place. The grounds were spacious and the foliage green and plentiful in comparison to Delhi. Santiniketan is in the midst of a rice-growing area, and a short walk brings you out of that island of higher learning into the land of rice paddies and small villages.

Sometimes in the evening a friend and I walked out to a village and along the ridges of earth that divide one rice field from another. In some places the rice fields stretch for miles, creating a feeling of great vastness. There, I felt, was beauty.

Tagore wrote of this place he loved:

Undulating, uninterrupted . . . spaces spread on all sides of this Santiniketan ashram. Here and there bushes rise sparsely, consisting of stunted wild palms, wild blackberry trees, a prickly plant or two, and anthills. Through these lonely fields a red streak of a path goes winding towards the villages on the horizon; along this path wend the villagers to the (market) at Bolpur town—Santhal girls with haystacks to sell, and loaded bullock carts whose moaning wheels leave a trail of dust in the silent sunlight of noonday. On the highest point of this leafless solitude, as can be seen from far, rises a row of tall, straight sal trees, through whose leafy foliage a traveller can glimpse the spire of an iron temple and a part of the roof of a two-storied building. Here, in a grove of mangoes and amlakas, amidst sal and mahuya trees, is our Santiniketan ashram.

Yes, as Tagore had hoped, we did live in close communion with nature. But as I became more familiar with Santiniketan's life I realized that, as in most universities, perhaps anywhere in the world, there was a lack of communion between the students and the *people* living in the nearby villages and the town.

I thought of Santiniketan as a kind of heaven in which everyone had enough food, a clean dry place to live, no hard physical work and no worries about where the next mouthful was coming from. I felt safe and secure at Santiniketan and lucky to be there. But we were surrounded by people whose lives were very different from ours, people who had to work hard, people who did not throw away half-emptied plates of food as some of the students did.

I felt a little uncomfortable in this atmosphere. It was not especially easy to enjoy the heaven while blissfully ignoring the many around us who could not share it with us.

TWELVE

Embroidery, Music and the Liberal Arts

THESE THOUGHTS while sitting at the temple and during the walks in the evening were part of my education and an important part as well. But there was another side of my learning which was perhaps more important, that is, my classes in the college and in the art and music schools. As I had been admitted at Santiniketan as a special student, I was able to take a course of study that included classes in the college and a little of both art and music.

Embroidery was the only course I took in the art school, Kala Bhavan. It was one of the many craft courses taught in that department, including weaving, leather work and batik, a type of cloth printing. The art school's main emphasis, however, is on Indian painting, design and sculpture.

I enjoyed the embroidery class, which met for two hours twice a week. There were five or six other girls in the class, all beginners like myself. We sat on the floor of a small unfurnished room in a building of the art school, cooled by the air that came in through the open windows and relaxed by the restful work we were doing.

We each had a big square of cotton cloth which we made, after a few months and with the help of our teacher, into a colorful sampler. By the time I left Santiniketan, I could decorate blouses, table mats and table-cloths and teach others the stitches I had learned.

I had two classes in the music school, tabla and Kathakali dancing. The tabla is a drum, in fact two drums which are played together. One, a higher-toned drum, is played by the right hand and the other, a deeper-toned drum, by the left. The tabla is sometimes played as an instrument in itself but is more often used as an accompaniment to other instruments or to singing.

Perhaps it was due to the facts that (1) I loved rhythm and the sound of a drum and (2) the tabla looked the easiest of the Indian musical instruments to learn, that I decided to study it. I was glad I had, although I soon realized that it would take much hard practicing to ever be able to play it well.

Our teacher was a Bengali, a tall, wonderful-looking man with just the right kind of fingers for tabla playing, long, lean and strong. Although I was no judge, I thought he played beautifully.

I was delighted when he, in showing us something, got lost in his own playing and played on and on. Closing his eyes, he would roll his head from side to side and tap his bare foot to the rhythm of the drum beat. I could never tire of listening to him—or watching him.

Our tabla class met for about an hour, three times a week. There were four or five boys in the class and two or three other girls. We met, sitting as usual on the floor, in a room of Sangit Bhavan, the music school.

In another room of the music school we had our Kathakali dancing class. Two main styles of Indian classical dancing are taught at Santiniketan, Kathakali and Manipuri. Kathakali is a fast, vigorous, rhythmic, very expressive style of South Indian dance-drama. Manipuri, which originated in Manipur, in northeastern India, is less vigorous and more graceful and flowing. Both of these styles of dancing are based on hand and facial movements.

Premkumar, a famous Ceylonese Kathakali dancer and the husband of one of my friends, an art school student, defined dance as the "outward expression of inward feelings through the medium of bodily movements." There were, he continued, two main mediums of expression, abinaya, i.e., facial movements, and mudras, i.e, hand and finger movements, without which the dance would have no meaning or beauty.

However, even without knowing the various mudras and their meanings, Indian dancing, especially Kathakali, was exciting to watch. When I should have been practicing myself, I used to watch different dance classes through the windows of Sangit Bhavan.

Because of its vigor and rhythm, I chose to learn Kathakali. Our teacher was a South Indian who danced expertly and beautifully. He was a perfectionist and soon became thoroughly annoyed with me because I could not devote several hours a day to practicing.

There were three other girls in the class. Our teacher started us with a lovely dance called the Puja (worship) dance. We danced to the loud and heavily accented beat of a rather large, convex-shaped, double-ended drum. The drum followed the dance exactly and the beat was suggestive of the dance steps. Like the tabla, each sound of the drum had a monosyllabic name, as "te," "re," "ki." We learned the "words" of the dance by heart.

After a month or so we began to learn the mudras, the various hand movements. There are twenty-four mudras, each having from two to thirty or more meanings. For instance, the first mudra is called Pathaka and with different forms of the Pathaka mudra you can portray a lion, king, sun, elephant and so on. It wasn't easy to learn these—I kept forgetting the first ones I had learned—but a good Kathakali dancer knows hundreds.

The rest of my classes were in the college. I took Indian history, Rabindra-literature (the study of Tagore's poetry, plays and philosophy), civics and botany and, for a short while, history of Indian art and Bengali.

Indian history was the most interesting of the courses for me. Our teacher was a scholar in this field and was sincerely anxious that his students learn as much as possible. Unlike some of the other teachers, he was always happy to answer our questions thoroughly after class.

We began with a rather long and very helpful introduction explaining the absence of Indian written history, sources of Indian history, geography of India and so on. We then learned of the political and cultural history

of the country beginning with the year 2500 B.C., when
the civilization of Mohenjodaro is believed to have thrived
in what is now West Pakistan.

Indian history, like the other college courses, was taught
through lectures. Like the classes in Delhi Public School,
there was no discussion and few opportunities to ask
questions in class. We took notes and were advised to
read books from the library for extra information.

Indian history and the two civics courses which I took,
economics and politics, were held out of doors under the
trees. We sat on small mats on the ground, the students
in a semi-circle and the teacher in the front. I liked being
able to feel the breeze in the heat of a summer morning,
the warmth of the sun on my back on a cold winter day,
to hear the murmuring of the trees, and birds singing
above my head.

Next to Indian history, I liked the course in Tagore's
literature and philosophy best. This course was attended
mainly by non-Bengalis. Our teacher, who was an au-
thority on Tagore, stressed that less than five percent of
Tagore's works has been translated into English or were
written in English in the first place. Therefore he was
anxious to read Tagore in Bengali. When I left I had just
reached the point where I could read and understand
simple poems in that language.

It was delightful to listen to our teacher read the
poems in Bengali. They were musical—rhythmic, soft
and flowing. Even the English translations of much of
his poetry, are, I think, beautiful (and I am usually not a
poetry enthusiast). Here is a selection which I like:

The fire of April leaps from forest to forest
Flashing up in leaves and flowers from all nooks and
        corners.
The sky is thriftless with colours,
The air delirious with songs.
The wind-tost branches of the woodland
Spread their unrest in our blood.
The air is filled with bewilderment of mirth;
And the breeze rushes from flower to flower, asking their
        names.

There were only a few students in the Rabindra-literature class, a Punjabi girl, an American boy, a boy from Ceylon, another from South India, Okelo from Kenya, and myself. It was an afternoon class and the last of the day for some of us. So we often sat and talked for hours, sometimes very much off the subject. This class was more informal than any of the others. We each took turns reading and there were questions and discussion.

Our class was held on the porch of an old building which housed the college offices and a reading room for college boys who lived in a hostel nearby. A small tea shop was within shouting distance and each afternoon, during our after-hour discussions, we ordered cups of tea for each of us, and then perhaps, as the afternoon wore on, still more.

Ashokda, our teacher, was a wonderful person, kind and cheerful, and he often helped me to understand particular poems or passages in his spare time. I was so happy when he and the rest of the class presented me with three small books by Tagore, two in Bengali and one in English, when I left the university.

The rest of my courses, botany and civics, were, I imagine, similar to those of the same name in any part of the world. The botany class met four or five times a week in a well-equipped laboratory. The twenty or so boys and girls in the class were first year students, many of whom knew only a little English. As a result, the botany teacher often taught in Bengali. In the two civics courses, economics and politics, there was the same language problem. But our textbooks were in English as very few have, as yet, been printed in Bengali and the other Indian languages.

My economics teacher, with whom I had many disagreements, described America as a capitalistic country and then described the characteristics of capitalism in the following prejudiced terms:

   (1) there is private property
   (2) production takes place for profit
   (3) no village is self-sufficient

(4) there is great inequality of incomes; there are a few rich people and many poor

(5) it is the owners of capital who decide when, how and what to produce

And in our economics book it was written:

The evils of capitalism have caused its overthrow in Soviet Russia where the working class rules and has established the socialist system of production. Under socialism workers are not hired by capitalists but are employed by the state which owns all means of production and operates them according to a carefully drawn up plan. The results of production . . . are distributed to the people in an equitable manner. . . .

One night our economics teacher gave a talk to the university students on the economic system of the United States. It was obviously biased and unfair. Luckily there was a question period afterward at which one of the two American boys was able to correct the false impression my teacher had created.

I ran into this anti-America attitude seldom at Santiniketan. My father's contacts with Indian university students in various parts of India, however, showed him that many of them are suspicious of the economic system of the U.S.A. and of the foreign policies of the United States government. In view of their long and bitter experience with western colonialism, their suspicions were human and understandable. But my father felt that in many cases misunderstanding and poor information had biased their thinking and that they were anxious for the honest information which he gave them.

For the most part, however, the girls at Santiniketan did not talk and perhaps did not often think of these things. I expect that some of the boys would have expressed different views had I known them better.

Whatever their views on America, whether they disliked or liked what they knew about it, did not, I think, affect my fellow students' attitude toward me. Nalini, my best friend at Santiniketan, told me her suspicions of the sincerity of the policies of the United States government and her distrust of the American people generally.

Because Nalini based her opinions of the American people simply on the few Americans who visited Santiniketan, who, we agreed, were not always representative of the American people, I urged her not to be anti-American. I think she had great faith in her own people, people like our anti-American economics teacher, and found it hard to suspect them, yet easy to suspect foreigners.

In September of 1952, Nalini told me that she was suspicious of the burst of good will America was showing toward India. She could not understand why the American government was offering so much aid. There must, she felt, be some reason for it other than pure good will, and if it was, as she suspected, to persuade India to take the side of the U.S.A. in case of a third world war, why didn't the American government come out and say so.

Once she spoke of the prejudice against Negroes in our country. She mentioned that there were "a hundred some lynchings last year," and was not ready to believe me when I told her that lynchings were rapidly becoming a thing of the past. The Communists do all they can to spread such falsehoods among the Asian students.

THIRTEEN

New Friends

As my second month at Santiniketan passed by, I found I was beginning to get discouraged. I had hoped that the Santiniketan girls, if only because they lived in the "abode of peace," would be quiet, simple and hard-working. But I soon realized that whenever girls get together, in America or India, they are generally the same. Santiniketan provided fewer exceptions than I had hoped for.

However, this disappointment, which stemmed from a too sudden dose of carefree and outspoken girldom in the Kala Bhavan dormitory, was short lived. It is only a small part of my memory of Santiniketan, of the many good friends I had and of the wonderful times we had together.

The girls of the Kala Bhavan dormitory represented almost every province of India. At least a third came from Calcutta or somewhere else in West Bengal. There were also girls from Kashmir, the Punjab, Delhi, Uttar Pradesh, Madhya-Bharat, Bombay, Hyderabad and Assam. Two had come from Ceylon, Samira from Iraq, and Edna, who was studying music and dancing, from the United States.

The most commonly heard language was Bengali. However, although they were urged to learn it, the non-Bengalis, like myself, usually knew little Bengali. Among themselves they spoke either Hindi or English. With the Bengalis they spoke English.

The girls were generally very attractive. Their features were clear cut, their skin clear, eyes deep, dark brown, teeth a beautiful white, hair, long and jet-black and always neatly oiled and braided. Most of them were slim and graceful.

Their clothing, usually a plain cotton sari and blouse, was simple and added to their grace. The saries were white or modestly colorful pastel shades—green, blue, pink, yellow or violet, becoming to the girls' dark skin. Some of the girls wore simple sandals—most walked barefoot.

There is much to an Indian girl's makeup. The oiling, combing and braiding of her hair is a chore. Many of the girls applied blacking to accentuate the lines of their eyes. Some wore a red dot on their forehead and the married Bengali girls put a red streak in the part of their hair. But despite the fact that an Indian girl probably spends as much time before her mirror as an American girl, there is a certain freshness and simplicity about the Indian girl. Somehow you feel that the beauty she has is entirely her own.

It did not take long before I was accepted as a member of the dormitory and no longer regarded as a newcomer and a stranger. Many of the girls were extremely reserved when they first met me. With other girls, however, I was at once on warm and friendly terms.

One of these, Vijoya, was wonderful in helping me get settled into the Santiniketan routine. She and I were both sixteen, the youngest girls in the hostel. She was enjoying the first year of a four-year art course.

Vijoya's home was in Calcutta and her mother tongue was Bengali. In addition she spoke Hindi and English. One of the first evenings I was at Santiniketan, we took a long walk to the Calcutta-Northeastern Bihar railway line, the eastern boundary of the University, and Vijoya gave me my first lesson in Bengali. As we sat on the bank above the tracks, she told me that the Bengali language has a slight similarity to Hindi and six or seven other Indian languages because of their common root in Sanskrit. Sanskrit, a member of the Indo-European family of languages, is no longer spoken in India.

It was pleasant there on the bank. A slight breeze was blowing and it was cool. A train went slowly past while we were sitting there, the compartments bulging with people. We waved as it puffed by on its long uphill ride.

The monsoon had not yet ended and there had been rain in the early morning. But in the afternoon the clouds had vanished and the sun shone brightly in the blue sky. When we started back the sun was just setting.

Vijoya and I went on many other walks in the evening. She was full of fun and had an unlimited amount of energy. She usually wore a lovely flower in her hair.

I liked each girl in the Kala Bhavan dormitory for different reasons. I liked Vijoya for her spirit and good-naturedness. One of the girls I like tremendously but never came to know very well was Soma, a Ceylonese girl. She was older than most of us in the dormitory and married to Premkumar, the well-known Kathakali dancer of whom I spoke earlier. She was beautiful—tall and slender—quiet, friendly and kind. I never heard her angry.

However, most of my real friends were in Siksha Bhavan, the college. Of these I liked Nalini best. Nalini was a Punjabi girl, husky, strong and attractive. Unlike many of the girls, she was independent and outgoing. She and her family had lived in West Punjab, in what is now Pakistan, before partition. In 1947 they had fled to India and made their home in Delhi. Nalini's mother tongue was Punjabi and she spoke in addition, English, Hindustani, and a little Bengali learned since she came to Santiniketan.

Although this was her first year at Santiniketan, she was in her third year B.A. She and I had a few classes together. Nalini shared my interest in the villages and their people, and also my disappointment at the lack of connection between our life at Santiniketan and that of the nearby villages and the town.

Not long after I arrived at Santiniketan, Nalini, Vijoya and I took a walk westward from the dormitory past a shallow lake, flooded rice fields and a few faculty homes, along the main dirt road that connects Santiniketan and Sriniketan, a rural development center about three miles away. A mile or so along on our left was a small village, consisting of eight or ten small thatched-roof mud huts clumped together on high ground amidst the rice fields.

It was the middle of the monsoon and as we walked down the village's one street, it began to rain. We asked a small, dark-skinned woman if we could take shelter in the shed of her courtyard. "Certainly," she told us, and we went into the small room and sat down to wait for the rain to stop.

The shed was clean and dry. A calf was munching hay in a stall in the corner. There was a wooden plow lying on the earthen floor and various tools and big straw baskets hung on the walls and in the rafter. We stayed a half an hour or so, singing and talking, until the downpour had ended and we could head back to the hostel.

The people living in the villages around Santiniketan are either Bengalis or Santhals (pronounced Shāntāl). We were in a Santhal village. It is disputed whether the ancestors of the Santhals, a short dark-skinned people, were Dravidians or belonged to an aboriginal group that, it is thought, inhabited India even before the Dravidians. At any rate, it is known that they were some of the first inhabitants of India, driven to the jungles of Bihar, West Bengal and central India when the Aryan invaders came about 2500 years before Christ.

Living in the jungle this way, shut off from outside

contact, their way of living and some of their customs have remained almost unchanged. They are, today, among the most primitive of the Indian people. Of course the Santhals around Santiniketan have been in close contact with the Bengali villagers for some time and also have been somewhat influenced by the work Sriniketan has done. But they are still a clearly separate group.

One holiday, shortly before I left Santiniketan, Nalini and I visited a Santhal village in the early afternoon. The narrow street and the small homes were almost deserted. A few children were playing in the dirt, and on the porch of one of the houses two girls were busy pounding grain. They were shy but friendly. Although we could not understand one another's speech, we told them in sign language that we would like to help them.

The object was to remove the husks from the grain and their method was ingenious. A handful of grain was put in a cup-shaped hole dug in the earthen floor of the porch. A heavy wooden board with an attachment that fitted into the hole was fixed in a kind of see-saw arrangement. When you pushed down on the near end of the board, the far end which fitted into the hole went up in the air. When you let go it fell heavily into the hole, cracking the husks. It was tiring work.

Almost all of the other houses were closed and locked. In one of the few that were open we found a middle-aged woman sitting in the courtyard grinding grain, a young grandson playing nearby. In Bengali we asked her for water and were surprised when she responded in the same language. She told us that she had learned a little from her menfolk, some of whom had worked with Bengalis and Biharis as laborers in the season when there was little or no work in the rice fields.

Her home was clean and cool. There were no windows and it was dark inside. She kept drinking water in a decorated clay jar.

Where, we asked, were all the people of the village? Most, she said, had gone into the market at Bolpur. A few of the men were working as laborers. She was friendly and happy to have company. But we left after a short while and walked slowly back through the then dried and sunbaked rice fields.

My other best Santiniketan friend, Manjit, was a Punjabi refugee too. Manjit's home was in the northeastern corner of the Punjab, near the great Bhakra-Nangal canal where her father was working as an overseer.

Manjit was a quiet, earnest girl. She wore clothes of hand spun cotton as did most of the people at Sevagram, and plaited her thick, coarse hair into a single long braid.

Manjit, like Nalini, wanted to work for her country. However, I found during the summer when I visited her home, that her mother is an understanding but orthodox woman. For a young girl to travel nine hundred miles alone to school, is, quite naturally, a new and frightening idea to her, and it is even more unusual to have a daughter who has the outlook and ideas that Manjit does.

Manjit wished to do village social work and is well suited for the task. But due to her mother's opposition, she felt sure that in the end her life would run much the same as for her Santiniketan classmates—B.A., marriage and from then a home to be tied down to and confined in.

For a few months during the winter, from the end of our last class until it became dark, a few of us practiced track events together. We hoped that in January we might go down to Madras to take part in the annual all-India university athletic meet. This meant a long train journey, more than 24 hours each way, and spending two or three nights in Madras. We looked forward to it as a real adventure and a happy diversion from books and study.

I practiced the discus (I had come in first at the Delhi Secondary School Olympics). The others practiced running, throwing the javelin and pole vaulting. Unfortunately the administration took little interest in our training, despite our and our coach's enthusiasm, and when the time came to go to Madras, although we had practiced faithfully, we girls were told we could not go.

Of the two other girls working at track, Deepali was the one whom I came to know best. Each day we did exercises together. Then, while I practiced the discus, she practiced "starts," had one of the boys time her running and helped the boys with their practicing.

Deepali was a second-year college student and was lots of fun to be with. We were both very disappointed that we could not go to Madras. But we saw off the four boys who were going, at the Bolpur station, garlanded them with flowers and wished them good luck. They wired back as soon as the meet was over that none of them had shone in the events but they were having a good time.

Our coach, Subodhda, was a lithe, attractive man who was sincerely interested in training each one of us as best he could. He so inspired Deepali and me that for a while we got up at 4:00 or 4:30 in the morning to do exercises on the flat roof of the hostel. It was a beautiful time of day, dark when we first got up and light by the time we went for breakfast. But the early rising made us awfully tired by lunchtime and both Deepali and I gave up after a little while.

We had a few small admirers who watched us and often begged to help us in some way. One of these, not so small, was Mishtuni, a thirteen-year-old girl who was studying in the secondary school. Her father was the assistant registrar of the university and they had a home on the campus. Mishtuni's mother, Umadi, did craft work in her spare time and the small house was pleasantly decorated with hand woven cloths, embroidered pieces and batik.

I was anxious to learn batik and Umadi kindly offered to teach me. So for a month or so I went almost every afternoon or evening to Mishtuni's house and we sat on the floor, did batik together and talked. (Because Mishtuni spoke very little English and I little Bengali, our talking was rather limited.)

Mishtuni made a couple of handkerchiefs and I made a big tablecloth and some smaller mats. After Umadi had taught me the technique she told me I could come to their house any time to work on batik. So for a while I became a permanent fixture in their home.

To do our batik work, we drew a design on a piece of plain, light-colored cloth. The design could be done in two or three colors. The tablecloth that I made, for instance, was white, yellow and blue. On the part that I intended to leave white I first applied wax. Then the cloth was dyed in a yellow dye, the wax remaining. When the cloth was dry, I waxed the parts that I wished to remain yellow. Then the whole piece was dyed blue and the wax removed. It was fun to do and the results were lovely.

Mishtuni had three sisters, one away from home at the time, Madhusri, a lovely serious girl in the college, and Tuku, who was very little and as lovable, playful and spoiled as any small sister.

A very different person from Mishtuni and Madhusri was Ram Pravesh, a Bihari from the steel mill town of Jamshedpur. He was, unnecessarily I think, extremely pessimistic about the future of his country.

"With so many rich landowners in high government positions," he once said, "land reform will go through much too slowly. Without complete land reform the full development of India will never be achieved."

It is true, land reform was moving slowly in India. But I could only disagree with Pravesh's extreme pessimism. The important thing was that land reform programs were going through. Now the pace is more and more reassuring.

Although I disagreed with many of the things he said, perhaps I liked Pravesh just for the reason that he was interested and thoughtful about the future of his country. Pravesh had worked as a laborer in a Jamshedpur steel mill, a rare thing in India where too many students avoid manual labor.

Although most of the students at Santiniketan when I was there were Bengali, there were non-Bengali students from almost every part of India and from Ceylon, Nepal, Burma, China, Indonesia, Germany, Turkey, Iraq, Egypt and Kenya, Africa. Most of the foreign students were postgraduate or research students and we in the college rarely saw them.

Thomas Okelo, the boy from Kenya in Africa, was in the college and I came to know him well. He was tall and husky, had a beautiful face and a lovely soft voice. He told me a little of his country, enough to make me feel impatient until the day I might go there.

Vijoya, Nalini, Manjit, Deepali, Subodhda, Mishtuni, Pravesh and Okelo, were, I think, my best friends. But there were many other people at Santiniketan whom I came to know well and now that I am many miles away, remember often.

FOURTEEN

Extra-Curricular Activities

LIFE AT Santiniketan with my friends was by no means all work and no play. In fact a good proportion of our time was spent in having fun together. Almost every night there was either some kind of a "function"—a play, a music and dance performance, a lecture, or an informal get-together—or perhaps a picnic.

Because I attended classes in each of the Bhavans I was urged by my classmates to take part in each of the Bhavan "functions." So whether the lecture or entertainment was for art, music or college students, I would be included.

There was a picnic at least two or three times a month. There were all-day picnics, moonlight picnics, afternoon tea picnics and early-in-the-morning picnics. The biggest and best, held one hot day in September, was an all-day picnic for college students and faculty.

About a hundred of us left the school soon after breakfast on foot, along a small dirt road which runs past Santiniketan between Bolpur and the village of Goalpur, our destination. The heavy monsoon rains had washed out the road and the creaking bullock carts that we passed could hardly make their way. Lush green rice fields spread far on either side of the road, dotted here and there with palm trees and a small village or two.

Goalpur is a medium-sized, clean and picturesque Bengali village. Our picnic spot lay on its outskirts. A shallow, muddy creek, where cattle drank and water buffalo and village boys bathed, ran past the shady, grassy grove which we made our headquarters.

First food preparations and preparers were organized. The preparation of an Indian meal, even in a well-stocked kitchen, is no simple affair, but the organizers had planned to give us the best. Some of the girls set to work peeling the mountain of onions and potatoes which had been heaped in a convenient shady place. Others washed the rice and prepared the meat and dhal, and the boys made the fires. A bullock cart had brought our food and the pots and pans from the school kitchen, and some of boys drove it into the village to get well water.

While these preparations were going on, groups were organizing for play and singing, and by the time I had finished helping diminish the pile of onions, games of ringtoss, cricket and charades were well under way. One group was playing cards. A group of girls was singing and dancing. Another was listening to songs from the boys and girls in the group. And some of the boys were swimming in the creek.

We were all very hungry by the time one of the girls, clanging a metal spoon against one of the big brass cooking pans, announced that our lunch was ready. We sat cross-legged in rows on the grass. Our places were marked by big round leaf plates which were soon filled with steaming food—rice, dhal, potatoes and onions, and meat for the non-vegetarians. A mishti, a Bengali candy, followed. After throwing away our plates, which, with the leftovers, were soon consumed by the crows and bullocks, we settled down to rest.

We spent the remaining part of the afternoon watching an almost continuous comical drama, an on-the-spot invention of some of the boys which included singing, dancing, clapping, acting and speeches. It was done in Bengali but it was so obviously nonsensical that we all enjoyed it, Bengali or not.

Toward the end of the day, ringtoss and cricket started up again and just before we left, as the sun was going down to lighten the west, we had tea. Then a happy, singing procession headed back to school and the day ended with the singing of *Amader Santiniketan,* Our Santiniketan, the school song.

More common to Santiniketan than the picnics, however, were the "functions." A "function" could be any kind of a performance—a play, a ceremony, or a music and dance show. One of the "functions" I enjoyed most was a musical performance consisting entirely of folk dances and songs.

The building in which the classes of Sangit Bhavan are held lies around a big courtyard. One of the inner sides of the building is open to the courtyard. This forms a big stage, the courtyard serving as the auditorium. Here we sat on the grass, the starlit sky overhead, fully able to enjoy the cool breeze which was welcome in the hot night.

Most of the items of the performance were folk dances. The majority of these were stick dances, danced by some twenty or more boys and girls. The girls were dressed in bright purple, red, blue and yellow silk saries which they wore as full, ankle-length skirts. They wore light-colored blouses, bright shawls, big white or yellow flowers in their sleek black hair and lovely garlands round their necks. Interspersed between them were the boys, plainly dressed in white with orange turbans and waistbands.

Each dancer had two sticks. On every beat of the music there was a loud clap as these were hit together, either one person's stick against another's, or the two of a single person together. The dance started slowly but toward the end it became fast and excited. There were many versions of the stick dance; one was something like the grand right and left, the girls moving in one direction, the boys in the other, weaving in and out.

Another item of the program was an "orchestra piece," a folk tune of the hill people of western India. Although combinations of instruments are almost unheard of in Indian classical music, this piece was played by several instruments together. The sitar, a lovely sounding stringed instrument, was joined by two violin-like instruments called esrajs, played with a bow, a harmonium, flute, tabla and dholak, another type of drum.

Another night there was an informal get-together of the post-graduate and non-Indian students. Every continent except Australia was represented and we heard songs and poetry from almost every corner of the world.

The first item was a classical Bengali song sung by an Indian girl, a postgraduate student of philosophy. She sang slowly in a clear alto voice. Then came some African folk songs by Okelo, the college student from Kenya. His songs were soft, light and lively, sung in Luo, his tribal language.

Guvan, a Turkish student, sang us a Turkish song. Mantra, a tall, attractive post-graduate student from Bali, sang an Indonesian song, and there were more Indian songs. Lastly, after recitations in French, German, Sanskrit and Bengali, one of the American boys sang a Bengali song, accompanied—to the great amusement of his Indian friends—by his guitar.

August 7th, the date of Tagore's death anniversary, was a day of solemn festivities and many visitors at Santiniketan. From suppertime far into the night of the day before, the girls in the Kala Bhavan hostel had been busy stringing the lovely little white and yellow flowers they had gathered during the day into garlands.

It was always the job of the art students to arrange the decorations for the "functions." They were thoroughly happy doing their work and I, too, in helping them. Six or seven of us crowded into one of the girls' rooms and sat on the floor and on the bed to do our work. Singing and talking we put flowers in our hair and hung the completed garlands round our necks.

Our day started at 4:30 in the morning with a procession in the full moonlight through the Santiniketan grounds. We walked along slowly, singing a continuous repertoire of Tagore's songs, and watching the dawn as it came lazily over the horizon, followed by the sleepy sun. Once every month, when the moon was full, we went on these moonlight singing processions.

Later in the morning a commemoration service was held in the temple. In the late afternoon the main function of the day, a tree-planting ceremony which attracted many visitors, took place. It was unusual to see Santiniketan so noisy and crowded.

At the appointed time, a long line of girls, my hostel-

and class-mates, made a procession into the blocked-off area in the center of the crowd where the planting ceremony was to take place. Dressed in bright yellow saries and white blouses, they carried small plants or bunches of flowers.

In the center of this area, a big alpana had been made by the art students. An alpana is a design made on a hard surfaced floor or hard packed ground with a rice powder and water paint. Most alpanas are white but this one had red and yellow in it also.

The ceremony was in Bengali, so I could not understand all of it, but what I did understand was colorful and lovely in its simplicity.

In contrast to these quiet festivities was a four-day vacation in nearby Calcutta, India's largest city. Another American girl and I took advantage of holidays at the end of January to visit this metropolis. She was a student of Antioch College, at Santiniketan for only a few weeks.

Our lives at Santiniketan had run unbelievably smoothly. But as soon as we stepped outside the gate, uncomfortable questions arose. Somehow it was good to be faced with these decisions, good to be out in the world again.

We could take the train from Bolpur. But how would we get from the school into the station? A rickshaw wala had seen us standing outside the hostel with our sleeping rolls and suitcases. He stood waiting nearby, his three-wheeled cycle ready.

We had both vowed never to use a rickshaw pulled by a human being, vowed never to use another person as a mere beast of burden. This time, however, we could see no other solution. There was plenty of time but the road to town was long and the luggage was heavy.

To the rickshaw wala, a hardworking, Hindi-speaking Bihari from the province next door, our decision meant perhaps a little more food for his family at dinner time that night. We put our bags in and climbed up.

It was 1:00 in the hot afternoon and the few people we saw along the paved but dusty road were resting.

Within a short while we had arrived at the small,

crowded Bolpur station. We paid the rickshaw wala his well-earned fare, bought our third-class tickets to Calcutta and sat down to wait at a counter where a man was selling tea and sweets. The great majority of train passengers in India, especially the students, travel third class. The hundred miles into Calcutta cost us less than three rupees, or only about sixty cents.

About an hour later, the train steamed into the little station, tired and puffing after its long journey from the hilly north. We found our way into an already overcrowded compartment. It was intended to seat sixteen but there were many more—students, families, businessmen and a soldier. At Burdwan, the next and only stop, we were joined by frightened rice smugglers.

The police were looking for them and they were not welcome in our compartment. They were taking rice into the city where it could be sold for a higher price. They hopped off just on the outskirts of Calcutta when the train slowed down, and fled quickly before they could be seen.

As my friend was a talkative person, we were soon discussing the problems of the world with three students from Calcutta who had been at Santiniketan for the day. One of them, a boy from the north central province of the Punjab, was studying law. The other two were studying medicine. One was a Punjabi and, like the law student, tall and fair, as is typical of men from his part of the country. The other boy was from the neighboring mountain country of Nepal and was smaller and even fairer than the other two.

It was just getting dark when the lights of Calcutta came up before us and we crossed the Hoogly River bridge and rumbled into the Sealdah station. Despite the fact that the partition of India had taken place over five years ago, there were still religious conflicts in East Pakistan, and at that time Hindu refugees were pouring into West Bengal. For many of them their first Indian home was the Sealdah station. They waited there, huddled in family piles on the floor, until the government could provide them with places in camps or colonies. We walked past them and out into the cool night.

I was amazed. I thought we had come to New York. Trolleys, buses and taxis honked past and neon signs blinked at each other. Swanky tea shops and restaurants lined the main streets. I was silenced by the bigness of it. Quiet Santiniketan seemed a long way away.

The three students, with nothing but time on their hands, hired a taxi for us and left us at the Salvation Army hostel where we had heard we could get cheap room and board. It was cheap—three rupees per day, including food. Some old Anglo-Indian women and a few working girls, Indian, Anglo and Chinese, were living there. My friend took a room with a Punjabi woman who taught school and a young Indian nurse. My single roommate was an Anglo-Indian woman, old and poor.

The Anglo-Indian women in the hostel, like most of the Anglo-Indians I had met in Delhi, were strangely proud of their Englishness and did everything they could to be English. Dressed in Indian clothes they could so easily have been taken as Indians and welcomed into the Indian community. But they did not seem to want this. Most wore western clothing, spoke only English and hesitated to become part of the new India.

The three students left with a promise that they would be back to take us to supper. Before long they returned and we ate in a place where I, in my simple cotton clothes and well-worn sandals, was almost ashamed to go. Except for its beturbaned waiters and a few variations in the menu, it was similar to any of Chicago's plush, rug-floored, more modern restaurants.

Our hostel was a small, three-storied building on one of Calcutta's busiest streets. During the day the sidewalks beneath our windows were thronged with men and women. Dressed in somber white, they bargained in loud voices at the small shops or quietly discussed the state of the world as they walked hurriedly to work with companions.

The small, dark shops sold everything, from clothing to pots and pans. Little open-air stalls were set up on the sidewalk selling tasty fried foods, rich Bengali sweets, fruit and ice-cream.

Occasionally a bullock ambled its privileged way along

the road. Trolleys rumbled past, clanging their bells to clear a path through the crowded street. A tired rickshaw wala cycled slowly along, looking for passengers. Cars honked by, inevitably in a hurry.

How different from quiet Santiniketan. But although I missed the peaceful slow pace of Santiniketan life, our few days in Calcutta—where many, many people live the hurried lives of city people—were somehow refreshing.

No, life at Santiniketan was by no means all work with no play. I can remember so well how terribly I felt that day at the end of February, 1953, when I said goodbye to my friends and headed back to Delhi.

I realized then, however, that I would miss not only the good times of my Santiniketan life, but the everyday things too—the going to classes, the studying hidden behind a book shelf in the quiet library, the washing of clothes in a pail in the cement wash room, and the feel of the hot sun as I hung them out to dry. I would miss the peculiar sensation of freedom in having perpetually bare feet. Especially I would miss the gaiety and grace of the girls, and perhaps, even their noisiness.

FIFTEEN

Villages of Progress

I CAME HOME to Delhi from Santiniketan at the end of February. Steb, Chet, Sally and Sam were leaving India to return home to America in March. I wanted very much, and my parents allowed me, to stay in India for a few months longer to see more of the country and learn more of village life.

From the time my family left until I was to leave at the beginning of July, I would have over three months. Already invitations from friends would fill them. Jean Joyce, an American friend of ours who worked in the

United States Information Service in Delhi, and Sushila Nayar, a friend of Steb's, the Minister of Health and Rehabilitation in Delhi state, offered to be my "temporary guardians."

My family left Delhi near the end of March, 1953, soon after the hot, dry season of India's north had begun. Many people were at the airport to see them off on their trip home across the Pacific. We watched as their plane lifted itself noisily off the ground and flew gradually higher and higher.

I was alone then, but alone with friends in one of the friendliest countries of the world. I felt happy that I had the opportunity to stay in the country and with the people I had come to love so much. The following three months were to be the most enjoyable part of my time in India. I would be staying with several Indian families, families of different economic standing and religions.

For the next few days I was to be with my "temporary guardian," Sushila Nayar, and her family in Old Delhi. Sushila Bahen was a close disciple of Gandhiji and spent much time at Sevagram with him. One of India's leading physicians, she served Gandhi for years as his personal doctor. Before her appointment as state Minister she was for some time Chief Medical Officer at a large refugee colony near Delhi.

Like many officials of the new Indian government, Sushila Bahen studied abroad. She spent almost two years in the United States and received her master's and doctor's degrees in public health at Johns Hopkins University.

Because Sushila Bahen was busy during the day, I spent most of my time while staying at her house seeing my friends, working at the clinic in New Delhi and visiting the bazaars, "window shopping." There was much to do and I had little time to think about my family. Sushila Bahen was my temporary mother, a wonderful one. Shakur at 17 Ratendon Road also took great interest in my welfare. I visited him and the other people in the compound almost daily when I finished at the clinic.

I stayed with Sushila Bahen until the end of March. My next home was to be that of an American missionary couple, the Wisers, in a small town in Uttar Pradesh.

After I had returned from Santiniketan, I had talked with an American friend who, knowing of my interest in the villages, suggested that I spend some time with the Wisers and the colleagues of the organization they directed, the India Village Service.

"The Wisers," she told me, "live in a very small town called Marehra about a hundred miles southeast of Delhi in Uttar Pradesh. They would be glad to have you with them." She said that she would be going to Marehra herself the end of March and could take me with her. "Moreover," she continued, "one of their colleagues is working alone in a village near Lucknow, farther north in Uttar Pradesh, and would welcome help and company for a week. You could go there from Marehra."

I had eagerly accepted the invitation. At Marehra and the village near Lucknow, I would be able to see some of India's fast-growing effort at village development. India Village Service is a private organization but the work it is doing is typical of work being done all over the country by both private and government groups.

Everything worked out as we had planned. It took us just a few hours to drive to Marehra. Most of the way Uttar Pradesh's western plain, proudly bearing fields of ripe grain and pulses, stretched on either side of the road. The harvesting had begun and some of the fields were already empty. Everywhere the village people were busy threshing and gleaning the harvest.

My new hostess greeted us warmly. She and Mr. Wiser urged me to feel at home and to spend my time as I liked.

Marehra is what one in North India calls a kasba, not a big village nor a small town, but of a size between the two. Before the partition of the Indian sub-continent into the two independent countries of India and Pakistan in 1947, the town had been predominantly Moslem, but at the time of partition the majority of the Moslem population had fled in fear to Pakistan. Hindus and Moslems were being incited against each other, and in unthinking frenzy Hindus were murdering their Moslem neighbors and Moslems were killing their Hindu friends.

However the Mohammedans were afraid not only for

their lives. They were afraid, too, and as it turned out unnecessarily afraid, for their future. Many feared that India would become a Hindu-dominated state in which there would be discrimination against other religious groups.

Actually, I learned, there was no disturbance in or around Marehra. But throughout most of North India, as in Pakistan, many thousands were killed. Today, miraculously, Hindus, Moslems and Sikhs live together in India, for the most part in peace. Much of the credit for this miracle belongs to Prime Minister Nehru who has worked hard to bring all the religions together. Today the 45 million Moslems in India are among Mr. Nehru's most enthusiastic supporters.

The crumbling brick houses of the Marehra streets, with their tall, arched doorways, tell of days that were rich, at least for the more privileged. A Marehran woman, whom Mrs. Wiser knew, told me of a time she was small when an upper-class woman would not touch a foot to the ground outside her own courtyard. Carefully curtained palanquins, carried on the shoulders of four bearers, took her everywhere.

With the departure of most of its population, Marehra has become something of a ghost town. The narrow bricklaid streets are almost always deserted except in the early morning when small boys hurry along to school and men go about their business, and at sunset and sunrise when the men came to answer the bells of the mosque, the Moslem place of worship. The brick buildings, rarely showing a cheery face in their doorways, give a decaying and lonely atmosphere to the town.

The exception is market day, every Thursday, when craftsmen, farmers and buyers from miles around meet at the edge of the town. The men buy and sell but they do not go quickly away. It is a good opportunity to meet with their comrades and talk and joke for a while.

My host and hostess lived in an old Moslem home. There was a small courtyard at the back, encircled by rooms on three sides and the wall of an adjoining house on the fourth. My room was one of the two small ones at the back of the house, open to the courtyard where I slept. A common room and a porch were at the front of the house, the Wisers' bedroom, a kitchen and bathroom off at the side.

The house had been simple and the Wisers had kept it that way. The walls were crumbling brick, the floors in the back rooms were of dirt, my bed a charpoi. I wondered how it had been in the days before partition when a Moslem family had lived there. Probably the women of the household had spent most of their time in the two back rooms and courtyard, for the Moslem women in this area observe strict purdah. To keep men other than those of their own family from seeing their faces, they never go outside their homes without wearing the burkha, a shapeless, baggy garment which is worn over the regular clothing and covers the entire body and face.

I quickly made friends of two Moslem sisters who lived next door, one my age and the other a little older. One day when I was sitting in their courtyard, talking with them, the water boy, his goat-skin bag full of water from the nearby well, came in. While he was busy filling the clay jars, he kept a cover in front of his eyes so that he could not look at the girls and the mother of the household.

These girls and their older brother were lonely. Most of their friends had gone to Pakistan and there was little in their home or town to lift them out of the routine of daily household chores. I told the girls that I was working in the villages around Marehra and asked them why they did not spend some of their time doing work like that. I stressed the fact that I worked only among women and children. They smiled shyly at each other and told me simply that it was not their custom.

The town of Marehra has two schools—an elementary school for both boys and girls and a secondary school for boys only. There is a small, poorly-equipped hospital.

One afternoon Mrs. Wiser and I were invited to a ladies' tea party at the home of the doctor's wife in back of the hospital. The town postmaster's wife, the school teacher's wife and other of the more "educated" women of the town were there. Conversation, although carried on in Urdu, was much the same as that you might hear at a tea party of women in the United States—whose child had been born, who had died, who had recently been married, what was the price of vegetables, and so on.

While at Marehra I worked in the nearby villages with Violet, a young Indian public health worker, one of the seven or eight colleagues of the India Village Service. We spent a morning in each of the five villages, going on our cycles soon after early breakfast and returning by 1:00.

We offered our help where we saw a need and a desire for learning. If a small boy had sore eyes we taught him how to treat them. If a girl had a plain scarf and wanted to decorate it like mine, we would teach her and her friends embroidery stitches. If a person in the village had recently died of, say, typhoid, we would teach the sanitary precautions that should be taken to prevent typhoid, and so on.

Although the India Village Service is supported by the Presbyterian Church in the U.S.A., its activities, like those of the missionary group in South India, are related to Christianity only insofar as these activities are based on completely Christian principles. The colleagues, all of whom are Christians, speak of Christ only when they are asked by the villagers, or when a particular situation can be well explained or interpreted by a Bible story.

The organization's main objective is simply to "assist village citizens to realize the best in their own villages." By living the Ten Commandments and giving and working according to Christian principles, the members of the organization earn greater respect for Christianity than any missionary bent only on converting people could possibly do.

Like village extension workers all over India, the I.V.S. workers sought first to win the villagers' confidence, second, to initiate small improvements in the tools and farming methods of the village people, and third, to organize cooperatives, health services and schools with the help of the villagers and only when they are prepared to make the organizations successful.

In the I.V.S. villages much progress had been made. Violet proudly pointed out the new concrete wells in the villages and, outside the villages, a tube well, a deep well worked by a power pump which can irrigate as many as four hundred acres. She showed me also a field of wheat in which the farmers had sowed regular seed in the traditional way. Next to it, taller and healthier, was a field of wheat grown from improved seed introduced by the village workers. There were few who refused to use the improved seed at the next planting.

The village workers worked slowly, of necessity. There were no tractors, no combines, no complex machinery for harvesting, seeding or plowing. But small improvements had been made. The wheel of the bullock cart had been reinforced with steel for strength and longer wear and the village blacksmith had been taught how to make the part. The handle of the sickle used in cutting the grain stalks at harvest time had been made so that the blade cut closer to the ground and the user's knuckles were not bruised.

Plows had been built in the village which were lightweight and could dig deeper into the earth. Cow dung, which in the past had always been used for fuel, was heaped in compost pits and would be used as fertilizer.

Generally speaking, the job of my friend, Violet, and the other colleagues was to help others help themselves and to meet any recognized need in the particular villages in which they were working. Helping Violet with her job was a wonderful experience.

About a week and a half after my arrival at Marehra, in the second week of April, Mrs. Wiser saw me off on the crowded early morning train at the railway station ten miles away in the nearest town. I changed trains at Bareilly, reaching Lucknow in the early evening.

From the new, modern station I took a tonga to the Christian missionary college for girls, Isabella Thoburn College, on the farther side of the city. Here I met the India Village Service colleague who was working in Fatehpur, a village near Lucknow. We had planned that I would stay with her for a week.

We left immediately for the village, a walking distance of two miles. After almost a mile on the main road, we turned off and followed the railway tracks for a short way. From here, following a small path through a grove of trees, we came upon the Fatehpur village lane, small mud homes ahead of us and green cucumber gardens and a Persian well on either side. A small child playing in the lane spread the word that Bahenji had returned and men working in the fields greeted her warmly. "Bahenji aee hain!" Bahenji has come! Bahenji has come! the little ones shouted, so very happy to see their "elder sister" whom they loved so much.

Bahenji's home is on the edge of the village where the small lane from the town enters it. Made of mud, cow dung and a thatch-roof, it is no different from the other village homes except, perhaps, for its smallness. There were two small rooms, one in which the two cots and food cabinets were and in which Bahenji kept her books and clothing, and the other, a bare, open room, where we cooked and ate.

The little porch served as the village library where the villagers could come at any time to read the magazines and small books which Bahenji had received and wanted to share. A corner of the porch had been partitioned off by a brick wall and was used for washing. Although very near the city, there was no electricity in the village. At night friends sat together talking, sometimes singing, in the dark. Kerosene was expensive and people rarely lighted the kerosene lamps they had.

Early the next morning, Bahenji started at her work. A woman was sick in one of the first homes we visited. Bahenji advised her to go to the hospital and, in case she would not go, wrote out a prescription for some medicine which her son could purchase in the city. In the next house she helped a young woman cut out and sew some clothes for her new baby. In another she helped a small child with her reading, and so on through the village. This close, personal, friendly contact has helped the village people to develop confidence in her. Now, knowing they can always trust and depend on Bahenji, they come more and more to her for advice.

The work that she has done on literacy in the village is remarkable. One of the first persons whom she taught to read is now the village school teacher, teaching the younger girls and boys reading, writing and simple arithmetic. The older boys go into Lucknow city to school and the older girls, who can rarely be spared from the housework, come to Bahenji in their free time.

One of Bahanji's many projects was urging literate village people to write their own stories, simply and in their own dialect, which new literates could read and enjoy. Many of the people who have become literate lack books to read and will soon forget what they have learned if simple books which they can enjoy are not available to them.

Bahenji felt that, if the village people could get their own stories published, it would give the authors pride in being literate and provide an incentive for others to become literate. Moreover it would furnish a plentiful supply of books written in the language of the villager and on subjects in which he is interested and which he can understand.

Each day Bahenji and I returned around 12:00 for lunch. We rested in the hot early afternoon, and often some of the village women and girls came in to read with Bahenji, to sew or just talk. Late in the afternoon we again went into the village homes to talk and teach, returning soon after dark for supper. Afterwards, quite often, some of the village men gathered to listen to Bahenji's radio or the children played games in the lane that wound past the house. The night school met at that time too.

Most of the village men either own their own land or, more usually, work on someone else's land. A few work in the city. When I was at the village, the wheat and pulses had been harvested and beautiful crops of cucumbers, pumpkins, squashes and tomatoes were ready for the market.

One day one of my new-found little friends, Rajkumari, asked me to teach her some embroidery. We sat down at the edge of her father's garden on the bank of a small irrigation ditch. She frequently had to jump up to chase away the sparrows who were nibbling on the ripe fruit.

I taught the Fatehpur women embroidery and they taught me basketry, some of the loveliest I have ever seen.

They buy cheap dyes and dye the waste straws of their grain crops green, yellow and red. These they weave into lovely intricate designs. They use these baskets in their own homes and give them to friends and relatives as gifts at marriages and festivals.

Bahenji was earnest, hard-working and warm-hearted, perhaps the most purely Christian of anyone I have ever known. I wish one could find the good spirit she has created in Fatehpur in every Indian village. It is a new outlook on life built on the desire to move ahead.

SIXTEEN

Water from the Well

IN THE Rae Bareli district of Uttar Pradesh, southeast of Lucknow, is a small hundred-house village called Barkhurdarpur. No social worker or agriculturist has ever lived there. No village development program includes it within its sphere. This is the village in which Shakur was born and brought up and in which his family now lives.

I had met Shakur's wife and four children when they came into Delhi from the village shortly before I left for Santiniketan. Sabra, Shakur's eldest daughter, had been very sick and the family had come to the city to get a doctor's care for her.

Sabra had recovered and the family had joined Shakur in the small quarters at the back of our house and stayed with him through the winter. At the beginning of April they returned to their village where Sabra and her mother were needed in the harvesting work. But by the time Sabra, her mother, two brothers and sister had left Delhi, we were close friends and I had a warm invitation to come and stay with them at their home in Barkhurdarpur.

From Bahenji's small home at Fatehpur I took a tonga to the Lucknow Railway Station. Here I caught a train for Jais, the depot nearest Shakur's village. I travelled, as usual, in a women's and children's third-class compartment.

The compartment was crowded, mostly with Moslem passengers. Here in Uttar Pradesh many of the people, like Shakur and his family, are Moslem. The Moslem women are usually fair-complexioned and like so many Indians often very beautiful. Unlike their Hindu sisters, they observe strict purdah and only in their homes or alone with other women, as they were in the train, will they take off their burkha.

The distance from Lucknow to Jais was less than a hundred miles, but the train stopped frequently and it took us almost three hours. I had sent Sabra, who was just a little younger than I, a letter telling her of my coming. She, her uncle (her father's elder brother) and small sister, Kaneej, were at the station to meet me. I recognized Sabra's red chunni that she had worn so often in Delhi before the train had even drawn into the station.

We climbed into a small, two-wheeled, horse-drawn cart. After about three miles on the dusty, deserted and very sleepy road, we turned off through a green but dry mango grove on a bullock cart path which led to the village a mile away. The dry fields, recently harvested and empty, seemed to be thirstily looking forward to the life-giving monsoon, still more than two months away.

Sabra's house was at the far edge of the small village. An old brick structure, it was built, I think, by her grandfather as a young man. Sabra's mother was working in front of the open door when we arrived. She greeted me warmly as did her eldest son, Umtaz, age six. The youngest, Mumtaz, age four, was sleeping and, on being hurriedly awakened, was in no mood to even speak to me until sometime later when he was more thoroughly roused.

The only other member of the family was Sabra's paternal grandfather, a tall, gentle, aristocratic-looking old man with a flowing white beard. All his sons except the eldest were working, like Shakur, in different cities in mills or factories or in private homes as servants. Their families were with them. The eldest son, Sabra's uncle who met me at the station, is a farmer, the only one keeping up his father's lands.

Sabra's grandfather is a small landowner. That is to say, he owns a bit—three acres—of arable land. Although a tiny holding, it is more land than most of the people in the area possess. Most are landless laborers and receive a small percentage of the harvest in payment for their work.

To say that Sabra's grandfather is a landowner by no means implies that he is rich. But in his land and his two bullocks he has security. In normal times he and other such small landowners live not unlike the landless peasants of the village. But in years of drought or pestilence they will undoubtedly suffer less.

Most of Sabra's house was a big open courtyard where we slept at night, sat in the early morning and in the evening when it was cool, and in which Sabra's mother put the grains and fruits to dry under the hot midmorning sun. In a corner of the courtyard was a small earthen fireplace where Sabra's mother cooked the food over a woodburning fire.

Small rooms around the courtyard were for storage of grains and the scanty farm equipment. Sabra was proud of the room she called her own. In it was a charpoi, her trunk and a small trunk for her sister and each of her brothers.

In the corner of the courtyard was a drain, leading outside to the lane, where we could wash and throw dirty water. As at Fatehpur, there was no bathroom, electric lighting or running water. The adjoining fields served the first purpose, a nearby well the latter. Electricity is now a hope of the near future. When Bhakra Dam, north in the Punjab, is completed in about 1958, many thousands of villages in the Punjab, Delhi, Rajasthan and Uttar Pradesh are expected to benefit from its hydroelectric power as well as from its irrigation waters.

However, we seldom felt the necessity of artificial light, electric or otherwise. It is dawn's work to rouse the sleeping villages with her dim, soft light. The sun was only climbing over the horizon by the time we had washed, rolled up the bedding and stood the cots on the porch, and Sabra had begun her house cleaning each morning.

Daily she swept the earthen floor, fed the chickens housed in an upturned basket in the courtyard, scrubbed the pots and pans left from the night before, and drew water from the well. I loved to share her work. She did it ungrudgingly and as a matter of course.

The younger children, who usually slept later than we, washed and ate some food which their mother had prepared from that of the night before while Sabra and I worked. With the children the two men of the household ate, then Sabra and I, and lastly, the mother, taking what she wanted of what the others had left. Then Kaneej and Umtaz were off to school and the men to their post-harvesting work.

Sabra and her mother and I spent the morning in various ways. Often there was grain to pick over and grind in the heavy stone hand mill. There was the midday food to prepare. Sometimes Sabra and I washed clothes or sewed together. Or if we did not work we simply sat and talked.

Neighbors dropped in frequently, especially when the news had spread that there was an American girl in Sabra's house. Most of them were curious and at first not even friendly. My skin was a different color, my hair was fair and relatively short. Rarely, if ever, had most of the Barkhundarpur villagers seen such a person. Quite understandably, to many of them I was only a curiosity, not a fellow human being who was to be greeted and talked to.

Some of the villagers, however, especially the girls of Sabra's and my age, greeted me in a friendly manner. The day I arrived, after I had greeted and tried to be friendly to a group of neighbors who had come into the courtyard to see me, Sabra had nudged me and suggested in a whisper that we go up to the little storage room on top of the roof with some of her friends.

The girl were curious too, but friendly, and asked many questions—where had I come from, why was I in

India, did I have brothers and sisters, was I married and so on.

Almost all of them, Sabra included, wore a tiny gold ornament in their pierced nostril. I remembered that Sabra had not worn one in Delhi and I asked if they had any special significance. Yes, they explained, we begin to wear them when we are ready to be married, when we are fourteen or fifteen years old.

Then they started talking about a girl in the village who was to be married soon and about another girl who recently had come back from her susral, her mother-in-law's house. She had told her friends that when she did not do the cooking and housework just right, her mother-in-law became angry and sometimes beat her. Sabra and the others girls decided they had best become good cooks before the time came for them to go to their mothers-in-law.

Although Moslem, none of these girls or their mothers wore the burkha in the village. They simply covered their heads with their chunnis, as I had long since learned to do, and as is customary among Indian women of almost all classes.

The medium of conversation between Sabra, her family and myself was that dialect of Hindustani spoken in Delhi. The Barkhurdarpur villagers spoke a more Urduized Hindustani which was sometimes hard for me to understand. I could follow only the general line of conversation.

In the morning Sabra's mother cooked the midday food. The children came home from school at about 10:30 and we ate when the hot and tired sun had almost reached the peak of the great sky mountain it climbed daily. The main food was the unleavened bread that is called roti or chappatie. Accompanying the bread was a highly spiced potato or egg or, occasionally, a vegetable curry. There was milk, too, for the younger children. Sometimes we had rice.

Unlike Fatehpur, vegetables were almost unseen at Barkhurdarpur. When a vendor did come, probably from a distant village, the prices he demanded were far out of reach of most villagers. Except for the very serious lack of fresh vegetables and fruit, the diet seemed satisfactory. There was enough food. And although the meals we had at Barkhurdarpur were cooked without variety, they were among the best I had anywhere in India.

After eating we rested for perhaps two or three hours. At five o'clock Sabra went to a neighbor's house to learn Hindi, reading and writing. One day Sabra's teacher complained of the lack of a doctor and a school for the older children in the village. She said to me, "Sister, when you finish your studies, come here and open a school and a clinic."

I assumed that she was comparatively well-to-do when she said her son was studying medicine in Bombay. She had the money and, as Sabra's teacher, the ability to open a school herself. I asked her why she did not do so. She had no real answer. She was used to having outsiders do things like that.

I doubt that her doctor-to-be son will return to the village to practice. He has seen the bright neon lights of the city and they appear to him now more attractive than the shimmering kerosene lamps of the village. This attitude is natural and is shared by young doctors all over the world, but unless he acquires the spirit of self-sacrifice so necessary in India's young people, he will only join the numerous, more highly paid city doctors. His village will continue to suffer.

After Sabra's lessons we usually went walking or visiting. In front and in back of Sabra's house were mango trees, their unripe, green fruit the object of a constant barrage of sticks and stones thrown by Umtaz, Mumtaz and other young children in an effort to make them fall to the ground. The green fruit was good in a bitter sort of way, like green apples. We made those that were knocked down and not eaten into delicious chutney.

Far in back and to one side of the house stretched empty fields, and to the other side in a clear place underneath the trees the harvested grain of Sabra's grandfather and other landowners was being threshed and made ready for the mill.

When the sun had sunk beneath the earth, we ate our evening food, arranged the cots and bedding in the open courtyard, bolted the door and were soon asleep. Sabra's uncle slept outside near his grain and her grandfather upstairs on the roof with Mumtaz.

There is no need to say how happy I felt living and sharing the work of this village family. Unfortunately it did not last long. On my fourth day there I contracted a painful eye disease, trachoma. Probably one of the many case of sore eyes I had helped soothe with saline eye washes in Fatehpur had been caused by trachoma and I had then infected my own eyes.

After trying one or two unscientific village remedies I decided to go to the doctor at the small government hospital at Jais, three miles away. I reached there with the help of Sabra's uncle, a borrowed bicycle and a pair of sun-glasses, also borrowed, and was treated, like the other patients free of charge, by the busy doctor.

I am afraid that my last three days with Sabra and her family were not as happy as the first. I was unable to open my eyes in the sunlight and therefore could not go outside Sabra's room. Worst of all, I could not help with the household work.

I left my Barkhurdarpur home and newest family reluctantly. I remember my week there as one of my very happiest in India.

Barkhurdarpur was a village untouched by modern ideas of farming and sanitation. In Barkhurdarpur there were no tube wells, compost pits, soakage pits or sanitary draining systems. The mouth of the well where Sabra and I drew water each morning was uncovered and level with the ground. Sticks and dirt were easily kicked in. The dirty household water was allowed to run out into the village lane. Sabra's uncle plowed, sowed and harvested as he and his ancestors before him had for centuries. And the success of the crops depended to a great extent on the precarious generosity of the monsoon rains.

I told Sabra's uncle about the sanitary cement drain and soakage pit many families in the I.V.S. villages had. "Yes, Bahenji," he said, "but to make one would cost money and take time. It would not be worth it."

This man lacks what the Indian government's Five Year

Plan calls "a progressive outlook," an outlook infinitely more desirable if success is going to be achieved in India's social revolution as I had seen it at Sevagram and the I.V.S. villages. I had seen this progressive outlook at Sevagram, in the villages around Marehra and in Fatehpur. But in Barkhurdarpur it was nonexistent.

It was nonexistent, too, in Bahenji's Fatehpur before she moved there. It was still lacking in some of the villages Violet and I visited. The village women were interested in no more than who I was and whether I was married. Even the children seemed to be infected with this "I don't want to learn" attitude.

In Barkhurdarpur a village worker would face the same problems the I.V.S. workers, the nurses at Chawla and village extension workers all over India were successfully dealing with. Fundamentally, the problem was a certain inertia and unwillingness to accept new and, to the worker at least, better ways of doing things.

On seeing this inertia, some people say with impatience, "It is no use. The people of the villages don't want to learn. To try to teach them anything is a waste of time. If they prefer to live and die in ignorance and poverty, let them do so."

Bahenji, Violet and the other colleagues of India Village Service look at it differently. Is it to be expected that a person will want to plant his crops in rows when he and his father and grandfather have always planted them helter-skelter? The farmer sees no advantage in planting systematically and times are usually too precarious to take chances with new and unproved methods.

That a person, whose only experience with a hospital is having heard of someone who went there and never came back, refuses to go to the hospital even when seriously ill, is natural. It is difficult to persuade cautious people of any nation of the importance of hospital care if they are ignorant of what it can do for them.

To a person who has never heard of a germ, clear water is sufficient evidence of clean water. How hard it would be, if you were not brought up in a germ-conscious culture like America, to believe that there are little tiny things, so small you cannot see them, that can make you ill. How easy it would be to blame your sickness on the gods as the people in Chawla had done when the little boy had become ill with typhoid.

Can you, Bahenji or Violet might ask, imagine yourself living in a tiny village surrounded by deep woods? The boundaries of your world are the boundaries of the village area. You have never gone outside this area, never seen any other way of living besides your own. Your grandfather, an old and respected man in the village, and the rest of the older men all farm the same way. Your grandfather's way is the way to farm. It would probably never occur to you that there might be another way.

Would you be easily convinced that there were not only other ways, but better ways? Wouldn't you be skeptical of any outsider who came and suggested you make any big changes in your farming tools and methods? You might not only be skeptical, but suspicious and even hostile as well.

The Indian villages have been slumbering for centuries and only now, with the independence of the country, are the people begining to awaken, to feel the need and desire for more than what their simple villages can offer them.

It is a big exciting awakening. By 1961, according to the Second Five Year Plan, every village in India will be covered by the agriculture, public health and education extension system. The core of the program for rural development is the community project. Already community projects serving some 100,000 villages, about 70 million people, have been set up in India.

A part of the Five Year Plan's program of rural development is the construction of several dams for irrigation and hydroelectric purposes. The largest of these is the Bhakra-Nangal project in northeastern Punjab. The father of my Santiniketan friend, Manjit, was an overseer on the project. Manjit invited me to spend a week with her and her family.

My trachoma cleared up quickly and I was soon able to accept Manjit's invitation.

Ten years ago, the area around Manjit's home in the dry foothills of the Himalaya Mountains, in upper Hoshiarpur district of East Punjab, was deserted save for a few scattered villages. Nangal, now a flourishing township, complete with its own schools, hospital and places of worship, simply did not exist.

After the partition in 1947, thousands of Hindus and Sikhs, pouring into East Punjab from Pakistan, came as far as Hoshiarpur district to try to make a living from the dry land. Today most of the refugees are employed —as engineers, overseers, drivers, mechanics and laborers— on the giant Bhakra-Nangal project, and the Nangal area resounds with the sound of machinery.

When I was there, the first stages of this tremendous project were nearing completion. When the dam, the power houses and the lattice work of the canals are fully completed, the dry areas of the Punjab will be entirely irrigated and enough electricity will be produced to light many thousands of villages in the northern states. This is the largest irrigation project in the world, and the largest dam is second in height only to our Hoover Dam.

The whole vast area will again be changed, to a fertile, irrigated land plowed by a people starting life anew.

Manjit and her family came with the stream of refugees, leaving behind them a comfortable home and secure life. Her father was able to get into government service and obtained employment as an overseer, like so many others, on the Nangal canal.

He and his family live near his work, actually ten miles south of Nangal alongside the canal. It was exciting to be awakened in the night by the roar of a bulldozer or truck, busy day and night at their work.

In many places convenient to the working operations, temporary quarters have been constructed, rent and electricity provided free to canal workers. The quarters were small for a big family, but satisfactory. In Manjit's home there were two small rooms and a storeroom, a tiny kitchen and a courtyard shared with a cow and her newborn calf. It was a lonely place, only a few families, nine dusty miles (the roads are temporary too) from the nearest town.

I stayed a week with Manjit. It was her summer vacation and we spent most of the time in the house, reading, writing, sewing and talking together. Indeed, the heat outside was not inviting. Once we went out during the morning to the nearby town of Nangal. Bustling with activity, the town houses almost all the workers on the project including some American technicians who are helping the Indian engineers on this, one of their first great engineering projects. Another morning we went to Khakra to see the beginnings of the dam.

I left Manjit and her family after a happy visit. A giant Sikh refugee driver offered to take me to the railway station in his truck along with a load of empty cement sacks. I reached Delhi in the evening.

SEVENTEEN

Idle After Busy Months

BETWEEN MY RETURN to Delhi from Barkhurdarpur and my visit with Manjit, I spent almost three weeks in Delhi while the trachoma cleared up. I stayed with my American "guardian," Jean Joyce, who lived with other Americans working in Delhi in a small apartment building in Old Delhi.

Jeannie worked during the day. So I spent most of my time at 17 Ratendon Road, visiting Shakur and the other servants who lived in the compound behind our old house. I usually went to see them in the morning and stayed the day, going to the doctor in the late afternoon. The men were on a half vacation, preparing for the arrival of the new American ambassador in India, Mr. George Allen.

The compound was a crowded one. Nine families lived in nine tiny, perhaps 8- by 15-foot homes, sharing a common courtyard and bathroom. But despite the crowding and the religious and language differences, they all lived together peacefully.

Shakur, a Moslem, lived alone now that his family had

gone back to the village. His mother tongue was Urdu. Kishorelal, a young, good-natured man, a Hindu, lived with his wonderfully cheerful wife and four children.

The cook, Sushen, and his wife were Buddhists who came originally from East Bengal. I called Sushen's wife Didi, meaning "elder sister" in Bengali, her mother tongue. A very attractive woman, she wore her hair, always neatly oiled and combed, pulled back in a bun at the nape of her neck.

Jewan, the driver, and his wife, both older people, were Sikhs whose village home was in a community project area in the Punjab. Their mother tongue was Punjabi. Jewan's wife was a gentle, kind, motherly person. "As my daughter is," she said me one day, "so you are." She wore the Punjabi pajama-like salvar and cumeez.

There were two gardeners, Hindus, both of whose families lived in villages in Uttar Pradesh. The older gardener's wife, a bold, fun-loving woman, stayed in the compound most of the summer. She wore the coarsely woven saries and heavy silver jewelry of a village woman. Her heavy anklets jingled musically as she walked. She showed Kishorelal's daughter, Shanti, and me the huge callouses that the rubbing metal had made on her feet.

Madan, the janitor or sweeper, lived with his young son and daughter-in-law. Like the gardeners, his mother tongue was village Hindustani. Madan was a Hindu untouchable. He did the dirty work of the household, scrubbed floors, emptied garbage pails, swept the porch and so on. While not treated in an unfriendly manner by the others in the compound, he was considered, merely because of the accident of his birth, unequal and inferior.

Just when I thought my family and I had made it clear that we looked upon each person equally, I was told by some of the children to be sure not to take food or water from Madan's house. Although in some ways we could help to create a greater equally among the servants during our short stay in India, two years could never overcome the prejudice of a lifetime.

Nisar, the watchman, was, like Shakur, a Moslem. Also like Shakur, his village home was in Uttar Pradesh. His wife and three children were with him only for a short while. He was a tall, bearded man, his face badly scarred by smallpox.

The washerman, Badri Prasad, his wife and three young boys, were Hindus. Their home was originally Agra, the city of the Taj Mahal. The washerman worked for two or three other families in the neighborhood besides ours. He did his washing in a big cement tub in his corner of the compound, a wonderful swimming pool for the children on hot days. His wife did the ironing with a big, heavy iron filled with red hot coals.

The children in the compound naturally became my special friends. Shanti (her name means Peace), Kishorelal's oldest daughter, a strong, pretty girl of thirteen, was responsible for watching her small brother and for a great deal of the cleaning and cooking. She had the loveliest long, thick, jet-black hair. It was a daily chore to comb it out and braid it neatly into a single thick braid.

Pyarelal, whose name means Lovable Ruby, Shanti's brother, was about ten. Each morning I would find him dressed neatly in white shirt and shorts ready to go off to school. In the afternoon, school clothes hung carefully in the house, he played with the washerman's two boys in the back alley.

Lila, Shanti's young sister, was six. Enjoying those happy days of gilhood when one can do almost as one pleases and dress without thoughts of modesty, she was as completely carefree as Shanti was responsible. She was burned dark from playing long hours in the hot sun wearing only a pair of shorts. Kishorelal's youngest child was six-month-old Ashok Kumar, chubby, cheerful and healthy.

Bhagwandas (Servant of God), the washerman's oldest son, was, like Shanti, about thirteen. Also like Shanti, he had responsibilities—helping his father with some of the washing and his mother with the ironing. Like Pyarelal, he attended school and almost every day proudly read his English lesson to me. Bhagwandas's brother, Babu Lal, about eleven, was a typically brow-beaten younger brother.

Ram Das was two, the youngest in the family. He was a sickly, weak, but lovable child. I was particularly fond of him. My mother had tried repeatedly to have the baby receive steady medical treatment. Unfortunately his parents, because of transportation problems and a distrust of the hospital, were unwilling to continue the treatment. The baby remained sadly weak and undeveloped.

Sometimes I wished that the children might never grow older and have to suffer the responsibilities of adulthood. They treated me as their big sister and to their mothers and fathers I was an adopted daughter or small sister. Shakur once told me, "I think of you as my 'chotti bahen' "—my little sister.

The hospitality of these people was unlimited. I was always urged to have lunch with one family, take the afternoon rest with another. A few times I stayed with Shanti for the night.

I tried to repay them, in some measure, by bringing candy and fruit for the children. I used my bicycle as a taxi, to the store, to the school and sometimes just for fun-rides with the children. When the women cooked I sat near to watch and help. But not all the gifts in the world could pay back all they gave to me. I could repay them fully only with my love and understanding.

In contrast to these days spent in the busy crowdedness of the compound was a week of leisure in a spacious summer home in Kashmir. Sushila Kahen had friends who offered to take me with them from Delhi on their yearly vacation trip to the mountainous north.

We left Delhi by train for Pathankot, the northernmost railway station in India. We reached there early the next morning and drove on by car to Srinagar, the capital and main city of Kashmir, 265 miles by road from Pathankot. We drove higher and higher up into the mountains, up to nine-thousand-foot Banehal Pass and then slowly down into the Srinagar valley.

We reached Srinagar in the evening in a cold and drizzling rain. The house lay outside the city proper, sitting on a wooded hill overlooking the main road. It was a quite big but barely furnished structure reminding me of summer houses in Maine.

The family with whom I was staying was a well-to-do Punjabi family who had lived in the Pakistan part of the

Punjab before the partition. The unquestioned head of the household was the grandfather, an eye doctor who remained busy at his profession even during his so-called vacation.

Both he and the grandmother were treated with great respect by the younger members of the family. The women always kept their heads covered in the doctor's presence and in the morning came in and bowed before him. The little children touched his feet. He rarely spoke sharply but he had a commanding voice and it was taken for granted that he was to be obeyed.

The grandmother was a small, greying, pious, gentle woman. She has a master's degree in Sanskrit, a most honorable achievement.

Also in the family while I was there were two daughters-in-law and their children, an older boy in his second year at medical school, three girls sixteen and seventeen years old, studying in Delhi high schools, and two small boys, six and four years of age.

This was an orthodox Hindu family. Among orthodox families such as theirs it is customary to have daily prayers in the early morning. Now only the grandparents have this worship service. ("The younger generation is forgetting its religion," the grandfather said to me.) Each morning they invited me to take part.

Sitting near a small wood fire, the grandfather chanted Sanskrit prayers praising God, taken from the ancient Hindu book, the Vedanta. At specified times during the reading he, the grandmother and I threw purified butter, water and spices on the fire. This symbolized the purification of the air, water and food. Often, at other times of the day, I found the grandparents in prayer.

Kashmir, "the Switzerland of India," is a summer resort for hundreds of well-to-do Indians and numerous foreigners and tourists. Unfortunately I was in Kashmir only four days and each day was rainy. So I had little opportunity to see anything of its beauty besides Srinagar city and the scenery on the way from Pathankot. But what I could see somehow disappointed me and I was not unhappy to return to the dry plains of the Punjab.

The Kashmiri people are known for their lovely hand

industries, especially their embroidery. The women and the three granddaughters of the family with whom I was staying often went shopping in the tiny clothing shops in the city. In the narrow, one-room, open-front stores, intricately embroidered saries, shawls, blouses and vests were hung in conspicuous places to catch the shopper's eye. Men sat cross-legged on the floor or on low wooden benches, busily sewing, trying to meet the demand of the summer tourists. While my friends were looking through the shop or haggling with the shopkeeper about a price, I tried to learn new embroidery stitches by watching the flying needles of the workers.

With my new family I passed four days of restless laziness and comfort. There were servants to do all the work. It was the women and children's job to sit and talk and lazily pass the time of day.

I could not be really happy in this atmosphere. Sabra's uncomplaining diligence and the extreme simplicity of her village home, the tireless work of the Wisers, Violet, my Fatehpur Bahenji and the other colleagues of the India Village Service, and the cheerful crowdedness of the compound at 17 Ratendon Road, were all too happy and fresh a part of my memory. I felt ashamed to sit and be idle.

EIGHTEEN

Welcome to the Punjab

VIOLET AND my Fatehpur Bahenji were Christians. Shakur's family were Moslems. The family vacationing in Kashmir were Hindus. Manjit and her family were Sikhs. Kaval, a girl I had known in Delhi, and her family were Sikhs too. With her for a week, at her home in the city of Amritsar in the Punjab, I learned more of this Sikh religion.

It had been over a year since I had seen Kaval when

she was studying in Delhi and, as I had never known her very well, I was a little apprehensive as to how welcome I would really be at her home. But I remembered the warmth of her invitation and realized that I should not have worried. She had written me soon after my family left India:

. . . It'll be wonderful if you come to Amritsar. You must come and must stay with us. I'm telling you the truth and nothing but the truth that the pleasure will be entirely ours. I shall be looking forward to your arrival.
. . . We shall try our utmost to make your stay a success and I sincerely hope you'll stay as long as your time allows. My uncle, who is my guardian, shall be your guardian too. I'm sure that you will like him.

Kaval and her uncle met me at the airport, some five miles outside Amritsar city proper, where I had arrived after a two hour flight from Srinagar. In Kaval's uncle's small car we drove to their old-fashioned, simple, brick home situated on a quiet street in the cantonment area on the outskirts of the city. One-floored, it was something like Sabra's house, only bigger, with a central courtyard and rooms around it. Unlike Sabra's house, there was electricity as there is in almost every city home.

Kaval introduced me to the other members of her large and exceptionally wonderful family only as we happened to meet them as she showed me through the house. In each there was abounding friendliness and welcome.

The eldest member of the family was the great-grandmother, Kaval's mother's paternal grandmother. She, the grandfather, grandmother and a great aunt, comprised the older generation and were more or less permanent members of the household.

When I was with them Kaval's mother's sister and brother-in-law (the uncle who met me) and her brother and his wife and small daughter made up the younger generation. Kaval, while at high school in Amritsar, was living under the guardianship of the uncle who had met me. Kaval's own family lived in Delhi.

Kaval explained that her Amritsar family was unlike most joint families. The head of the family was her mother's father and not her father's father as is usually the case. It would have been customary for her aunt, i.e., her mother's sister, to live with the family of her husband when she was married. Instead her husband had come to live with her family.

It is a family of doctors. The grandfather is a well-known and respected general practitioner in Amritsar. A fairly elderly man, he worked it seemed unceasingly, taking money only from those of his patients who could afford to pay him. Kaval's non-guardian uncle is an eye doctor and his attractive young wife a gynecologist.

The other uncle, Kaval's guardian, is a general doctor and lecturer at a private college for boys in Amritsar. His wife is the principal of the girls' high school in which Kaval was doing her pre-medical study. It was Kaval's guardian and his wife whom I came to know best.

The uncle, a kind, handsome man in his later fifties, seemed younger. An orthodox Sikh, he wore his greying uncut hair in a simple turban. Kaval and he seemed in many ways much alike. Both are aware of and interested in improving the existing social conditions. They are profoundly religious Sikhs, yet hold a deep respect for every faith. They are simple and informal, straightforward and sincere. I was happy that I could know them.

Kaval and I often had long talks together and perhaps no one has shared my ideas so completely. She is an attractive girl, tall and husky like most Punjabis. As fair-skinned as I, her hair is a rich brown color, just a shade darker than mine. Kaval has never cut her hair and two neat braids hang down to her waist. She wears simple cotton salvar and cumeez and, always, the single steel bracelet of the Sikhs on her right arm.

Kaval had gone to school at Woodstock, the American boarding school in northern Uttar Pradesh. There she had worn "frocks" and learned American slang, and when I knew her in Delhi she was a carefree, westernized teen-ager. Kaval left Delhi Public before I did to finish her schooling at Amritsar, an entirely Indian city. She had easily adapted herself to its simple life and had come to love it there.

When I was with her Kaval was studying a pre-medical

course and planned to become a doctor. She wrote me recently:

... I am planning to take up nurse's training as a Registered Nurse with the armed forces. My people are still keen that I should take up medicine but I feel that unless girls from good families start taking nursing as a profession its status in this country will never be raised.

and in another letter:

... India, or rather Bharat, has so much to achieve that it seems like a mammoth and completely impossible task. Yet we are progressing slowly but surely. I do so hope that one day I may be of more service to the people of India, my people, our people.

Kaval's simple daily life started with the first light of day, usually before 5:00. We had our breakfast of paratha and milk at about 7:30 or before Kaval left for school and her aunts and uncles for their work at 8:00. Lunch was at about 1:30 after everyone had returned, a lunch of the good food that makes the Punjabis among the healthiest people of India.

On the family table at mealtime there was always plenty of fruits and vegetables, curds and milk and a good-tasting kind of whole-grain wheat bread that was bigger and baked differently than the chappaties, parathas and puris I had had with other families. The food was delicious and I never felt shy about taking as much as I liked.

After lunch Kaval and I slept or talked until late in the afternoon. After a light snack of milk and crackers or sweets we went out—to the temple at the medical school, to a sports match or "sightseeing"—coming back in time for dinner at 9:00. Kaval studied and I read, or we sewed or talked until about 11:00. We slept—and it was always a good sleep—on the roof.

My days in Amritsar were altogether too short. During the time I was there, however, I was able to see some of the old, crowded city, the university and private colleges, and the pride of the Sikh people, called Hari Mandir or

Durbar Sahib in Punjabi and, in English, because of its gold-plated dome, the Golden Temple.

After I had left India Kaval wrote to me of her city:

. . . Amritsar is different from most places. Here there is no artificial social life, dances, late nights, etc. The whole atmosphere here, and especially at the Durbar Sahib (Golden Temple), is one of calm solemnity. The people of Amritsar are very religious though not fanatics. And as you know, wherever there's faith, love and harmony abide. That is how we are here, Cynthia, and perhaps all over India. I think that as long as we do not copy the Western countries we shall remain thus.

Amritsar is located in the northwest corner of the province now called East Punjab, not far from the Pakistan border. It is here in the East Punjab that most of the Sikh people are now settled, here and in West Punjab, now in Pakistan, that nine of their ten Gurus, or religious teachers, were born and preached their religion.

Sikhism, with only about six million followers, is best known in North India, especially in the Punjab and Delhi. Actually an offshoot of Hinduism, the religion has a likeness to Mohammedanism, Christianity and, in fact, as Kaval put it, "we have borrowed what we believe to be the good of all religions." The Granth Sahib, the Sikh holy book, praises God in the words of religious leaders and prophets of many faiths.

Guru Nanak, who lived around 1500 A.D., founded the faith in rebellion against both the Hindu and Mohammedan practices current in India at that time. He preached not a new faith, but pleaded only for brotherhood among the peoples of the different religions. "Love the saints of every faith," he said. "Not the shaven head. Not long prayers. Not recitations and torturings. Not the ascetic way. But a life of goodness and purity amid the world's temptations."

He denounced the caste system of the Hindus, "Nonsense is caste and nonsense the titled fame. God will not ask man of his birth, he will ask him what he has done." His words—"There is but one God whose name is true, the creator, devoid of fear and enmity, immortal, unborn, self existent, great and bountiful"—proclaim his belief in monotheism.

After Guru Nanak's beliefs had been established as the basis for the new faith, the symbolism which he had so loudly decried crept in. Today an orthodox Sikh should always have uncut hair and carry on his person a steel bracelet, a sword (this may be a miniature, inch-long), a comb (this also may be a miniature, stuck in the hair), and a certain kind of shorts. He must cover his head in public and in places of worship. The Sikh men comb their long, uncut hair up under a turban as Kaval's uncles did.

I went with Kaval and her uncle and aunt one night to the most famous of the Sikh temples, the Golden Temple. It is a place of pilgrimage for all Sikhs and many non-Sikhs as well, being the center around which Sikhism grew and first flourished.

The temple is a rather big building built within a very large water-filled tank. Yet it was not the bigness that impressed me. It was, instead, the devotion of the worshipers who thronged to the altar. Heads covered, we sat on the floor of a balcony overlooking the altar to listen a while to the hymns and watch the endless flow of people come in to worship and go out. Upon entering the temple a Sikh kneels and touches his head to the floor. At the altar the Granth Sahib, the sacred holy book, is being read and the worshiper walks around the altar, stopping to listen to the reading if he likes.

We sat for a long time but it seemed only a few minutes. I sometimes wish that I were now in Amritsar just so I could go and sit at the temple for a while each night.

I had visited temples before but in few of them had I experienced this atmosphere of quiet calm devotion. In a Hindu temple in Calcutta I had felt this same spirit of piety, yet to a lesser degree. It was a crowded, cluttered, dirty temple, erected for the worship of the goddess Kali, the main deity of a certain sect of Hindus. Devotees covered her image with flowers and coins. Others sat before the image, some in meditation, some as if entranced. The worshipers came and went and prayed as they liked.

Another temple we visited in Calcutta was an immaculate and very elaborate temple of the Jains. The Jains are a small religious community but well known in India for their asceticism. They believe in strict non-violence and non-possession, considering the taking of any animal life, however small, a sin. Some of the more orthodox Jains wear a cloth mask over their noses and mouths to keep from inhaling, and thereby destroying, germs.

The walls, floors and ceiling of their temple are beautifully designed cut glass and marble. It is not a big temple but in its elaborateness was unlike any other place of worship I had seen.

On our trip to Nepal we visited several Hindu and Buddhist temples. Originally the people of this remote mountain country were Hindus. In the third century before Christ, Buddhism was brought through the mountains from India by Ashoka, one of India's greatest emperors. Soon after that the Nepalese became predominantly Buddhist. Now, although the two religions, Hinduism and Buddhism, have, in many cases, become mixed and even confused, a majority of the people have returned to Hinduism.

Early one morning we drove to the foot of, and then walked up, the six hundred stone steps to the most famous of the Buddhist temples in Nepal, Swayambunath. Located at this temple, the object of Tibetan pilgrimages, is a Tibetan monastery, which we were allowed to enter.

In the semidarkness of the rather small main prayer room, about twelve Tibetan monks were seated in two rows on the floor, chanting from big, looseleaf sacred books, propped up in front of them. The twelve humming voices, all at different pitches, produced a delightful, though hardly melodious, drone.

In this temple, as in many we visited in Nepal and India, there was a little room on the walls of which was a series of pictures telling the story of Buddha. (In other temples the picture dealt with the divinity for whom the temple had been erected.) The room of this temple, besides showing pictures of Buddha, showed another amazing picture: Buddha, Christ on His Cross, and Gandhiji, grouped together under a caption that read, *Service to*

Humanity—a lesson to the world in respect for all religions.

There was a lump in my throat and a wish in my heart that we could meet soon again when I said my final "Sat Siri Akal" ("Truth is immortal"—the Sikh greeting) to Kaval and to every member of my new family, from the great-grandmother to the family servant, one beautiful June day. The grandmother's last words of advice to me were, "Khub paro. Ziyada vidhya pao." "Study well, acquire much knowledge."

NINETEEN

A Home Left Behind

THE END OF JUNE came quickly, much too quickly. My boat left early in July—I expected to hear any day from the American Express Company exactly when.

On the afternoon of Saturday, June 20th, I was out in the compound helping Bhagwandas with his English, Ram Das on my lap, when Shakur called me to the phone in the house. It was the American Express. A ship would be leaving for Marseilles, France, on July 2nd. I could take another boat from Genoa, Italy, arriving in New York the end of July.

The following morning, after last minute goodbyes to my friends, I boarded the Bombay train. Delhi was my home. It was hard to leave it and its people.

On the way to Bombay I planned to stop off for the day with a Parsi family, friends of the family with whom I stayed in Kashmir. Their home was in Jalgaon, a town in the Marathi-speaking area of northearstern Bombay state, just edging the Hyderabad border.

Late in the afternoon the southwest-bound train passed into the hilly uninhabited country of the Vindhya Mountains. It was just getting light the next morning when we reached Jalgaon and I was met by a boy and a girl about my age, two children of my Jalgaon host.

I spent an interesting day with the Parsi family. The father, my host, who had formerly managed a small liquor store, was out of business due to the new prohibition laws in Bombay state. His store building was in the process of being made into a hotel.

All of the family spoke a little English. Their mother tongue was Marathi, another sister tongue to Hindi. Their religion was Parsi. The Parsis follow the prophet Zoroaster who preached in Persia about 600 B.C. They originated as Zoroastrians in Persia. As the result of persecution they fled to India's friendly shore where they founded the Parsi sect. Today the Parsis are a small community settled primarily in the Bombay area.

The majority of the Parsis are highly educated and quite westernized. Many are successful businessmen. The dress of the Parsi men is distinctive. Those I saw in Bombay looked distinguished wearing a coat, trousers and a little round derby hat and carrying a cane.

The annual monsoon rains, which as yet had not hit Delhi, had recently broken over the Bombay area and the many small rivers in northern Hyderabad were flooded. My host and I cycled eight miles out of Jalgaon to the nearest of the these rivers. The crossing for vehicles was simply a slightly raised, paved road, a causeway, across the bed of the river. In normal times this was sufficient, but during the monsoon it is under from one to three feet of water. When we reached it, the first of a long line of trucks and buses, which had been held up for the last 24 hours, was just coming across. They plowed slowly through the fast-moving water which reached almost to the tops of the wheels.

From our side two farmers began to take eight or so cows and a few calves across. The swiftly flowing water caught more than half of them and they were swept off the road downstream, where they were eventually carried to one or the other of the banks.

"The monsoon," my host told me, "is looked forward to as a wet relief after three months of heat. But it turns usually dry rivers into torrents and often floods the low-

lying area before Bombay city. It rains almost daily here
and this river and the many others in this area will
probably become much more swollen before the season,
lasting usually about a month and a half, is over. Yet in
the spring months we will probably have drought."

My host's daughter, Perin, showed me around Jalgaon.
With all the conveniences of a fairly large town, it has
a women and children's park, a movie house and bazaars
selling everything one could possibly need. Right opposite
Perin's house is one of the town's two cotton mills.

Perin's little sister was studying in Jalgaon's primary
school. Besides the primary school there is a secondary
school, a government and a private high school, and
a school of agriculture in the town. At about 3:00, when
the schools let out for the day, the streets swarmed with
children—little ones walking soberly hand in hand, small
boys running here and there, teasing, playing with one
another, and laughing, neatly dressed teen-age girls, carrying stacks of books.

After lunch Perin and I went up to the second story
of their house where we could look down on the bustling
street from the porch. The majority of the people who
passed by were Marathis. Perin pointed out the free-
moving, neatly dressed women wearing green, red, purple
or blue, nine-yard saries, draped in a different, less becoming manner than that I had been accustomed to
seeing in Delhi.

There were Gujeratis too. The six-yard saries of their
women were draped in yet a different style. The Marwari
women from north central India were veiled and heavily
ornamented. Sindhi women, refugees from the southern-
most province of what is now West Pakistan, gave little
thought to the purdha which their grandmothers had so
strictly observed and were distinguishable by the salvar
and cumeez they were wearing as the Punjabi women do.

The provincial origins of the men were less obvious
from their clothing. Occasionally a Parsi gentleman passed
or a barefooted Jain, a member of that sect which believes
in strict non-violence.

I caught the Bombay-bound train soon after dinner,

arriving at Dadar, a suburb of Bombay, in the early morning.

Through the Experiment in International Living I had arranged to stay with a young Gujerati couple until my boat left. They lived in Matunga, another suburb of Bombay, near Dadar. Their home was a three-room flat in one of the many apartment buildings there.

The minute I met my new friends I lost all doubts about whether or not I was truly welcome. Malti Bahen, an attractive, pleasant woman, doubles as a good housekeeper and cook and an M.A. student of economics. Her husband is a young lawyer practicing at the Bombay High Court.

Due to the Bombay summer business and school hours which begin at 11:00 and continue until about 7:00 at night, the daily routine of Malti and her husband was somewhat different than that of most of the families with whom I had stayed. We got up each morning at about 6:00 and had some milk and maybe fruit at 7:00. Then Malti prepared the lunch which we ate early, before her husband left for work at 10:00. When I was with them Malti was not having classes. So after lunch we usually went out, either to see places of interest in Bombay, meet Malti's friends and relatives, or go shopping. We had a rather large tea wherever we were at about 5:00, and then returned home so Malti could prepare the dinner.

The food was delicious. I watched Malti cook whenever I had a chance and learned many things from her. She and her husband are strict vegetarians, excluding even eggs from their diet. Malti is a Gujerati Hindu, her husband a Jain from an orthodox Jain family. Malti told me that it was only after some argument that she was able to persuade her husband to let her kill the cockroaches that came into the kitchen.

Bombay is India's second largest city, both in area and population. It is not the regional city of any particular group of people but the southern boundary of the Gujerati-speaking area and the western and northern boundary of the Marathi-speaking area of Bombay and Hyderabad states. These two groups, the Gujeratis and

Marathis, combined form the majority of the population. But Bombay houses many other peoples of various languages, religions and provinces.

After partition Bombay opened its arms to many a weary refugee and now Sindhis and Hindu and Sikh Punjabis join their southern brothers on the crowded streets. Marwaris from central India and village people of Uttar Pradesh, who have come to the city to find work, form small communities.

In Bombay you find the Punjabis behind the wheels of the trucks and buses and in the garages working as mechanics. The working class people, most of whom have jobs in Bombay's many textile mills, and the intellectuals of Bombay—the writers, teachers and scholars—are mainly Marathis. The Gujeratis and Parsis run most of the shops and businesses.

Despite the fierce riots at the time of partition, Bombay is still the abode of many of the Mohammedan faith. It is the home of most of the Parsis. There are a few Christians and Sikhs as there are in almost every Indian city.

As you watch the flowing panorama of life on the crowded city streets, you are not sure in just which part of the vast country you are, so varied and different, in customs, clothing and language, are the people who go past.

The street language of Bombay is Hindustani. Being the national language it has taken its place as the common language in a city which is not even in a Hindustani-speaking area. In the streetcars and big double-decked buses, in which Malti and I went from one place to another, the conductors collected the fares in Hindustani. In many of the shops we bargained with the shopkeeper in Hindustani. And in the crowded bazaar, where Malti bought vegetables each night before returning home to cook supper, goods were bought and sold in Hindustani.

Malti and her husband were wonderful to me and I shall always be grateful for their efforts to show me the places of interest in the city. We knew each other little more than a week yet Malti seemed to understand my mixed feelings on leaving India. I was happy that I could spend my last week in India with her.

Tuesday, July 2nd, dawned a beautiful day, more beautiful than I had dared hope for during the monsoon. I wondered when I would see the sun rise over India again.

I was at the pier at 10:00, so that I could go through the usual red tape before the ship left at 1:00. Standing in line to have my passport checked, I no longer felt sad. Uppermost in my heart were apprehension and uncertainty about what lay ahead. Underneath this apprehension was, I was reminded over and over again during the long hours on the ship, a deep sorrow at leaving a land where I had learned so much, and for whose people I had come to have great love. But it was unrealized, unexpressed during the actual moments of leaving.

I boarded the big British ship at noon. Shortly after 1:00 the huge dock lines were cleared and the ship moved slowly into the Arabian Sea. Silently I watched the Bombay shoreline until it was out of sight.

Epilogue

I LIKE TO THINK of India as my second home. In no other place except Essex have I felt so strongly that I belonged. Someday, after I have completed college and specialized study in public health nursing, I hope to return to that second home.

After telling my friend, Suman, one day of my love for India and her people, she said, "You are young, and when one is young one wants love and a feeling that someone needs and appreciates you. We took you in and loved you. We welcomed you in our homes. You were needed and appreciated in Irwin Hospital and in the clinic. I question whether your love is really for India or simply for the love and appreciation which we gave you."

I feel that my love for India is more than a gratitude to the people who made me feel that I belonged.

Perhaps part of my love is for the simplicity of life and surroundings in Delhi, Chawla, Santiniketan, Marehra, Fatehpur, Barkhurdarpur, Nangal and Amritsar.

Part of it is for the color and beauty which I saw all around me, especially in the villages.

Another part of that love is an admiration for a country so determined to bring a better life to its people.

But perhaps the greatest part of that love for India is for my friends—Suman, Shakur, Nalini, Kaval and many others. These friendships have taught me not simply that East and West can meet, but that the very difference between the girl from India and the girl from America is not so great as is thought. Deep down, I realized, my Indian friends and I are very much the same.

Is it not the same with all people? It seems to me that it is only on the surface that people are different. The color of our skin, the language we speak, the food we eat, the clothes we wear—these external things are different.

Culturally, too, we are different. People live differently in India and America. They work differently and play different games. American standards of health, education and agriculture have little application in India at present. Even the values of right and wrong, good and bad in one culture cannot always be applied to the other.

These differing outside appearances, these differing standards and ways of living and doing things, and even of thinking, often appear as insurmountable barriers in the way of communication, of understanding and of friendship. But is there not something, besides the mere physical fact of our all being human, more basic and more important that is shared between all peoples regardless of the culture to which they belong? Are there not certain universal values and emotions which are common to us all? Is there not a great basic similarity that far outweighs the differences between the peoples of the world?

It seems to me that there is and I believe it is on this basis that true friendships can be made across cultural barriers.

A knowledge and awareness that most people everywhere share the same dreams would do much to further sympathy and understanding in the world. From understanding will come friendship. Our great hope is that from friendship will come peace.

GLOSSARY OF HINDUSTANI WORDS

CLOTHING TERMS

Chunni—A shawl-like cloth worn over the head or around the shoulders by women wearing salvar and cumeez.

Cumeez—A shirt.

Dapatta—Same as chunni.

Dhoti—A rectangular-shaped cloth worn in a variety of ways by men in India.

Khaddi—Hand-spun cotton cloth, often worn by people to encourage village industries.

Salvar—A pantaloon-like pajama worn by men and women in North India and especially in the Punjab.

Sari—A bolt of cloth, between five and nine yards long, worn in a variety of ways by women in India.

FOOD TERMS

Chappatie—Most common of several kinds of unleavened bread eaten primarily in North India.

Curry—Any spiced meat or vegetable mixture.

Dhal—A lentil-like legume, cooked in water and spiced.

Lhassi—A drink made from curds and water.

Pan—A chewing concoction of spices and betel nut.

Paratha—A fried unleavened bread.

Puri—Another type of fried unleavened bread.

LANGUAGES

Bengali—A language derived from Sanskrit, spoken in Bengal.

Hindi—A language directly derived from Sanskrit, spoken in Central India.

Hindustani—A combination of Hindi and Urdu.

Punjabi—A language derived from Sanskrit, spoken in the Punjab.

Sanskrit—An ancient language of India, member of the Indo-European family of languages.

Tamil—A Dravidian language, unrelated to Sanskrit, spoken in South India.

Urdu—A language derived from the Arabic, spoken in North India.

MISCELLANEOUS TERMS

Ahimsa—Doctrine of non-killing, non-violence.

Ashram—Literally, shelter.

Bahen, Bahenji—Sister. *Ji* is a suffix denoting mixed affection and respect.

Barat—The processsion in which the bridegroom comes to the home of the bride for the wedding ceremonies.

Bullock—Used in referring to any cattle in India, usually hump-backed.

Charpoi—A string-bottomed cot, very common in North India.

Gurdwara—The Sikh place of worship.

Lotah—A small brass jar-like container.

Mosque—The Moslem place of worship.

Mutka—An earthen jug.

Namaskar—A term of greeting in Bengal.

Namaste—A term of greeting in North India, accompanied by gesture of hands.

Tonga—A two-wheeled, horse-drawn cart, common taxi.

BOOKS